Abstract Data Types
in Standard ML

Abstract Data Types in Standard ML

Rachel Harrison
University of Southampton, UK

JOHN WILEY & SONS
Chichester • New York • Brisbane • Toronto • Singapore

Other Wiley Editorial Offices

John Wiley & Sons, Inc., 605 Third Avenue,
New York, NY 10158-0012, USA

Jacaranda Wiley Ltd, G.P.O. Box 859, Brisbane,
Queensland 4001, Australia

John Wiley & Sons (Canada) Ltd, 22 Worcester Road,
Rexdale, Ontario M9W 1L1, Canada

John Wiley & Sons (SEA) Pte Ltd, 37 Jalan Pemimpin #05-04,
Block B, Union Industrial Building, Singapore 2057

Library of Congress Cataloging-in-Publication Data

Harrison, Rachel.
    Abstract data types in standard ML / Rachel Harrison
        p.   cm.
    Includes bibliographical references and index.
    ISBN 0-471-93844-0
    1. Abstract data types (Computer science)   2. ML (Computer program
    language)   I. Title.
    QA76.9.A23H37   1993
    005.7'3—dc20

                                                                92–39975
                                                                CIP

British Library Cataloguing in Publication Data

A catalogue record for this book is available from the British Library

ISBN 0-471-93844-0

Typeset in 10/12pt Times from author's disks by Text Processing Department,
John Wiley & Sons Ltd, Chichester
Printed and bound in Great Britain by Dotesios Ltd, Trowbridge, Wiltshire

Contents

Preface

The aim of this text is to present a thorough treatment of data abstraction within a functional framework. The programming language used throughout is Standard ML, a functional language which is becoming popular as a language for teaching programming in both Europe and in the United States. The text provides material which is suitable for both software engineering courses (such as courses on advanced programming, program design, algorithms and data structures, and program specification) and also for intermediate and advanced level functional programming courses.

Standard ML, which is sometimes referred to as SML (or simply ML) is a standardised version of ML (which stands for *meta language*). ML originated in the late 1970s, primarily as a system for finding and testing proofs (Gordon *et al* 1978). There are a number of SML compilers available; the examples given in this book were tested using Standard ML of New Jersey, a compiler from AT&T Bell Laboratories. Instructions for obtaining the compiler are given in Appendix 2.

Throughout the book, we have stressed the importance of the concepts of specification (of both abstract data types and algorithms), encapsulation, modularity and generality. The approach to abstract data types strikes a balance between theory and practice. The importance of producing reliable, high quality code which is robust and reusable is emphasised. Each chapter shows how to specify, apply and implement generic abstract data types, and the specifications are used to verify and validate the correctness of the implementations. Although the philosophy of the text is the same as that of Harrison (1989), the contents have been completely revised: material which is not relevant has been omitted, the relevant material has been extensively rewritten, and a large amount of new material has been added.

FEATURES

The book incorporates a number of special features:

- The importance of correct specification and implementation (of both abstract data types and algorithms) is emphasised.
- Numerous annotated algorithms in Standard ML are presented.
- A wide variety of abstract data types are covered in detail.
- Exercises and worked examples are provided.
- A summary of the main points is given for each chapter.

PREREQUISITES

The main body of the text assumes some familiarity with a functional language, but the first two chapters provide some introductory material for readers who are only familiar with other programming languages or for those who wish to refresh their knowledge of functional languages. A detailed knowledge of the syntax of Standard ML is not necessary, as syntactic constructs which are peculiar to SML are explained as they are encountered.

SYNOPSIS

Chapter 1 introduces the key concepts of data abstraction, specification and functional programming. The reasons for using functional languages in general are explained, as are the reasons for choosing Standard ML in particular. The methodology of algebraic specification is introduced, and the use of asymptotic analysis as a means of analysing the complexity of algorithms is outlined.

Chapter 2 is slightly unusual, being the only chapter which does not demonstrate an implementation of its abstract data type. This is simply because lists are predefined in functional languages, and are usually not considered as abstract data types. Consequently, although we show how to specify the abstract data type list, we then go on to demonstrate a variety of sorting algorithms using predefined lists and pattern matching in the usual way. Finally, we show how functional programming facilitates reuse, with some examples of text processing.

Chapter 3 puts the theory proposed in Chapter 1 into practice, by showing how to specify, use and implement the abstract data type stack. The use of functors to implement generic abstract data types is demonstrated, and the advantages of such an approach are highlighted. Chapter 4 presents the abstract data type queue along similar lines.

Chapters 5, 6 and 7 follow the pattern of specification and implementation which was set by the previous chapters. These three chapters are all concerned with trees: algorithms for searching and sorting are discussed and analysed asymptotically. The usual terminology associated with trees is also introduced.

Chapter 8 is concerned with the abstract data type set. Sets are frequently used during the specification stage of the software life cycle, and by providing the abstract data type we can facilitate the prototyping and dynamic testing of such specifications.

In Chapter 9 we demonstrate how to specify and implement the abstract data type graph. The conventional terminology for graphs and directed graphs is introduced, and the access procedures are used to implement routines for searching, sorting and manipulating graphs.

Appendix 1 contains a collection of general utility functions which are used throughout the text, and which are written in Standard ML. Appendix 2 gives details of how to obtain the Standard ML of New Jersey compiler.

CHAPTER 1

Introduction

The importance of data abstraction as a software engineering methodology has long been recognised. This chapter gives a historical perspective of the methodology, and discusses the importance of using data abstraction to facilitate the development of high quality, reusable code. The use of functional languages is also discussed, and the reasons for using Standard ML in particular are outlined.

The high cost of software development has led to interest in the production of reusable software; in this book we encourage reusability via data abstraction, especially through the use of generic components. The type system employed by Standard ML facilitates the use of both polymorphic and generic software, and so a brief introduction to the system is included in this chapter. The method of specification of abstract data types is also outlined, as are the measures for efficiency which are used throughout the book.

WHAT IS ABSTRACTION?

The Concise Oxford Dictionary gives the definition of the verb *abstract* as 'to deduct, remove, consider apart from the concrete'. Wirth (1986) described the process of abstraction by saying: 'certain properties and characteristics of the real objects are ignored because they are peripheral and irrelevant to the particular problem'. Abstraction is at the very heart of all problem solving. It can be described as ignoring all unnecessary details and thus simplifying the task under consideration.

Abstraction can be used to decompose a complex problem into smaller, more manageable sub-problems. The difficulty of coping with large-scale software systems has been known for some time; in the sixties the term *the software crisis* was coined to describe the rapidly escalating costs of software as systems became increasingly complex. The structured programming revolution attempted to bring some methodology into the world of programming by suggesting elimination of uncontrolled jumps (*goto* statements) and use of only three control structures: sequence, selection and iteration. Following on from this, in 1971 Wirth coined the phrase *stepwise refinement* to mean successive decomposition of a task into several separate, less complicated subtasks. Abstraction facilitates simplification by providing a mechanism for separating the attributes of an object or event that are relevant in a particular context from those which are not.

Thus, abstraction is a logical consequence of the *divide and conquer* approach to problem solving which has been advocated as a problem-solving methodology ever since the study of software engineering began. Most programming languages facilitate (to varying extents) the use of two sorts of abstraction: procedural abstraction and data abstraction. *Procedural abstraction* refers to the use of procedures or functions to encapsulate and name a single task. *Data abstraction* refers to the use of abstract data types, as described in the following section.

DATA ABSTRACTION

In Guttag (1977) the term *abstract data type* is used to refer to 'a class of objects defined by a representation-independent specification'. This separation of specification and implementation is fundamental to the methodology of data abstraction. An implementation of an abstract data type (or ADT) can be replaced by another, provided that the replacement satisfies the original specification. This has the effect of protecting the implementation from the user, who is only given access to the ADT's specification. This separation of specification from implementation is extremely important, as it reduces the complexity of the system. Data abstraction is sometimes also referred to as *data hiding*. Before we can define the term ADT more precisely, we need to say what we mean by the expression *data type*. We will use the following definition:

- A *data type* (or *type*) is a means by which we can classify objects which have identical properties. A data type can be either intrinsic (built-in) or user-defined.

When using data abstraction, we are more concerned with *what* we can do with the data type than in *how* it is implemented. This leads us to the definition shown below:

- An *abstract data type* (or *ADT*) consists of a data type together with a set of operations, called *access functions*, which define how the data type may be manipulated.

These two definitions imply the use of a *strongly typed* language:

- *Strongly typed* languages are those which incorporate type checking systems such that all functions are required to be type correct: each function is defined to operate on objects of a specified type, and application of the function to an object of inappropriate type is flagged as an error.

Strongly typed languages (of which Pascal is a typical example) often allow users to define their own data types. Our definition of the term *data type* should be familiar to anyone who has programmed in such a language.

The term *data structure* is often used in the literature; we will define it as follows:

- A *data structure* or *structured data type* is an organised collection of data elements.

The terms *data structure*, *compound data type* and *compound types* may be used interchangeably. Data structures are created by using predefined constructors (such as lists and records in Standard ML) together with other predefined types such as int, string and `boolean`. User-defined data types can also be used to create data structures. Data structures can be considered to be at a lower level of abstraction than ADTs; they provide the supporting framework which can be used to implement ADTs. The main difference between ADTs and data structures is the formal specification of the access functions which should be provided by the implementor of an ADT. The access functions for data structures are provided by language implementors. For example, in Standard ML we can access the head of a list by using the function `hd`. Similarly, in Pascal, a field f_1 of a record `r` can be accessed by using a dot ('`.`'), as in the expression `r.`f_1.

Figure 1.1 shows a hierarchy of abstraction, with ADTs at the top and the machine-level representation of data at the bottom.

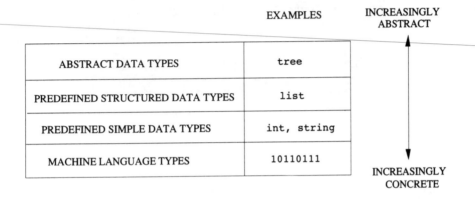

Figure 1.1   A hierarchy of data types

Data abstraction can be described as a method of expressing the interaction between a program and its data structures. This controlled access can be thought of as building a black box or wall around a program's data structures (see Figure 1.2).

The interaction between a program and its data structures is defined by the operations that describe the ADT. These are the access functions which are used to manipulate the ADT and they are the *only* way which the user of an ADT can interact with it. A program's result must be independent of the way the access functions for its ADTs are implemented.

The term data abstraction had become recognised as a programming methodology by the beginning of the eighties, and was hailed as the next leap forward in the evolution of software engineering. The influence of the data abstraction revolution can be seen in the design of several imperative programming languages, including Modula-2 and Ada, and this influence is continuing, with much research now going on into the design of *object-oriented* programming languages such as Smalltalk-80 (Goldberg and Robson 1983) and C++ (Stroupstrup 1985). An *object class*, usually abbreviated to *class*, is equivalent to an ADT, in that it can be considered to be some private data together with a set of operations that can access the data (Rumbaugh *et al* 1991). Many functional languages also provide various sorts of data abstraction facilities. Those provided by SML, in particular, will be discussed in more detail in the following chapters.

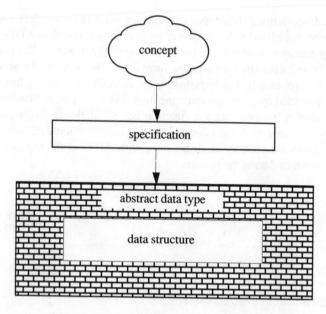

Figure 1.2

ADVANTAGES OF ABSTRACT DATA TYPES

We can group the advantages of ADTs under four separate headings.

The Code Produced is Well Modularised and has High Reuse Potential

An ADT can be thought of as a *black box* in that we can use it without worrying about how it actually works. We can draw an analogy between an ADT and a television set: a television can be thought of as a black box which we can use (by changing the channel, adjusting the volume, etc.) without needing to understand its internal structure. In the same way, we can use ADTs which have been provided by others without ever needing to know about their implementation.

ADTs are very flexible; once they have been specified, implemented and tested they can then be used and reused wherever they are needed. They form the basic building blocks for future software development.

A Reduction in the Complexity of the Software

Data abstraction allows us to concentrate on the desired properties of a data type and what it should do for us, rather than on *how* it should do it. As the size of software systems increases, anything which helps to reduce the complexity of large-scale software projects is to be welcomed.

The Independence of the Implementation is Assured

The separation of the definition of an ADT from its implementation means that there can be several equivalent implementations, giving the programmer the opportunity to change the implementation without having any effect on the rest of the system. This is particularly easy in languages which allow the physical separation of the definition of an ADT from its implementation (such as Modula-2 and Standard ML).

This independence of implementation gives us the added advantage of efficiency; if one implementation of the access functions is deemed to be too inefficient, it can easily be replaced by a more efficient version, without affecting the software which depends on the ADTs.

The Provision of a Specification

The specification of an ADT provides us with a formal definition which can be used for both verification (the formal, mathematical proof of a function's correctness) and validation (the rigorous dynamic testing of a function). Over the past twenty years or so computer scientists have become increasingly concerned with the need to produce software which has not only been tested but which has actually been proved to be correct in all cases. This is particularly important in the production of an air traffic control system for example, or a system to control a nuclear reactor. An increasing interest in verification has led to a lot of research on specification techniques, since there must be a correct and formal specification against which an implementation can be verified. By formalising the production of software we can hope to transform software engineering from an art into a science.

The specification of an ADT can also be used to help to validate its implementation. In providing a specification of an ADT we have given its semantics, which can be used as an *oracle* (Weyuker, 1982) to predict the expected results during the dynamic testing of the implementation. (Examples of this approach will be given throughout the book.)

The following section discusses the importance of formal specification in general and techniques for the specification of ADTs in particular.

SPECIFICATION

A specification of a software system is a detailed description of the functionality of the system. Specifications can be either formal or informal; the former is usually used at the designer–programmer interface, and the latter at the user–designer interface. Informal specifications are often produced in a form which can be easily understood by customers who may not have technical backgrounds: consequently, many informal specification techniques involve the use of graphics to some extent, and are well documented. For example, data flow diagrams are used in the Structured Systems Analysis and Design method, SSADM, a systems development methodology which is in use in the UK (Downs *et al* 1988). The specification at the designer–programmer interface must be unambiguous so that the programmers working with the implementation can understand and use it, always producing the same solution, whatever methods they employ. The use of a natural language such as English is therefore not sufficiently precise for this task; instead, a more formal specification is preferred.

Specification of ADTs

We will use an algebraic specification technique (Guttag 1977, 1978) to specify ADTs. This involves stating formally both the syntax (names and parameters) of the access functions and also their semantics (the rules which define their behaviour: the relationships between the functions and the way they can be manipulated). This is called an *algebraic* form of specification because the syntax of the access functions together with their semantics can be regarded as defining an algebra.

The syntax of the access functions can be defined by a list of function headings, and the semantics will be defined by a list of axioms. (An example of this technique will be given in the next chapter.) Algebraic specification is sometimes also called *axiomatic* specification. The technique falls within the broader classification of *definitional* or *implicit* specification because the behaviour of the functions is specified implicitly by definition, without any concrete representation (such as data structures and code). Jones (1986) calls this method *property oriented specification of data types*. For a description of a number of specification techniques for ADTs and a discussion of the importance of formal specification see Liskov and Zillies (1975) and Gehani and McGettrick (1986).

As mentioned earlier, the algebraic specification of an ADT gives us a list of axioms which we can use to verify all of the implementations of the data type. The construction of such a specification prior to any implementation is extremely useful not only in formal program verification but also in clarifying the details of the implementation. Ensuring that the implementation satisfies its specification enables us to guarantee its behaviour and reliability.

FUNCTIONAL LANGUAGES

This book describes the use of data abstraction within a functional language. There are several reasons for choosing to use a functional language, two of which are described below.

1. The Relationship between Specifications and Functional Programs

Functional programs are *declarative:* their semantics constitute a well-founded logic in which programmers can specify *what* the results of their programs should be rather than *how* to compute the answers. Consequently programming can be a simpler and more reliable activity.

The declarative nature of functional languages means that we can use the specification of a function to drive the development of code. Often, the relationship between a specification and a function is immediate and direct. For example, consider writing a function to sum the integers between the bounds `lower` and `upper`, where `lower` is less than (or equal to) `upper`. We can specify the function as shown below:

```
sum = lower + ( lower + 1 ) + ( lower + 2 ) + ... + upper
```
or

$$\sum_{lower}^{upper} i \; = \; lower + \sum_{lower+1}^{upper} i$$

Using pseudocode, we might write this slightly more formally as:

```
sum lower upper = if lower = upper then lower
                  else lower + sum (lower + 1) upper
```

This is very similar to the way in which the function would be written in a functional language such as SML; in fact, only the keyword fun needs to be added to produce an executable SML function:

```
fun sum lower upper = if lower = upper then lower
                      else lower + sum (lower + 1) upper
```

Because there is often a direct relationship between a function's specification and its implementation in a functional language, functional programs are often referred to as *executable specifications* (Turner 1985b). Algorithms can be explained very simply, without the need to spend time explaining peripheral details or discussing the logical errors which can occur in an imperative language, such as those which arise due to incorrect boundary values for loops, and so on. This direct correspondence facilitates the production of correct software, and is a particularly attractive feature of functional programs when compared with attempts to derive complicated iterative algorithms in imperative languages.

2. The Semantics of Functional Programs

Functional programs are mathematically tractable: they can be analysed and manipulated using well-understood mathematical techniques. Therefore program *transformation* (the systematic and rigorous derivation of efficient programs from initial specifications, as described in Darlington and Burstall (1976)) is possible, as is program analysis.

The interchangeability of two expressions which have the same meaning is called *referential transparency* (Stoy 1981). An example of a referentially transparent language which most people are familiar with is mathematics. For example, if we were told that the value of x is 3, and then asked to evaluate the expression:

$$5 - x$$

we would give the answer without a second thought. Since x and 3 denote the same value they can be interchanged. Referentially transparent functions can be reasoned about by using *substitution of equals*. Functions written in imperative languages, on the other hand, are often not referentially transparent: the values of variables are *history sensitive*, because they depend on what has happened previously in the program. For example, if we had a variable called x, say, which occurred several times in a program, and we happened to know that at one point in the program the value of x was 3, then we could not rewrite the program substituting the value 3 wherever the variable x occurred. This is one of the stumbling blocks to proving that code is correct if it is written in an imperative language. To ensure that functional languages are referentially transparent the use of assignment is restricted.

Many functions written in imperative languages are not referentially transparent because there are no restrictions on the use of the assignment statement and because of the use of *side-effects*, where a function which has a side-effect can be defined as one which has more than one effect during the course of its execution. An example of a side-effect is any change to a non-local variable. Writing functions with side-effects results in code which is very difficult to reason about, and so is more likely to have unforeseen consequences. For example, given a function sqrt to calculate the square root of a number we may assume that

```
sqrt (x) + sqrt (x)    = 2*sqrt (x)
```

If the function sqrt changed the value of its argument or of a variable used to compute its result then this relation would no longer hold.

The relationship between functional programs and their specifications, and the well-defined semantics of functions written in functional languages, have given us sufficient reason to choose a functional language as the paradigm used throughout this book. However, it must be admitted that functional programming has been criticised in the past as being extremely inefficient, both in terms of execution speed and memory usage. Such considerations are becoming less important, partly because the cost of hardware has decreased dramatically over the past 20 years (today's personal computers are cheaper and more powerful than many of the mainframes that were used in industry a decade ago), and also because a lot of research into novel machine architectures is currently in progress. Most computers which are in use today are based on the conventional Von Neumann architecture, with a single processor connected by a bus to an amount of memory. This design has not changed since it was first conceived in the 1940s. If programs are written in referentially transparent languages then different parts of a program can be evaluated in parallel, with processors working simultaneously, and this parallel processing may help to alleviate concerns over efficiency. Finally, research into the efficient compilation of functional languages is very much in evidence. The combination of these factors should provide further improvements in efficiency in the future.

Why Standard ML?

The language used for this book had to be able to support the concepts of data abstraction and modularity. SML has a very sophisticated module system, where a module is defined to be an encapsulated collection of functions. There are two different sorts of modules in SML: *structures* and *functors*. A structure is simply a collection of functions whose scope is limited by the start and finish of the structure in which they are implemented (for an example of a structure, see Appendix 1, which contains a library of utility functions). A functor, on the other hand, is a module which takes a structure as a parameter. An interface can be provided for both structures and functors in the form of a *signature*, which gives information about the types of the functions within the module. These facilities for modularity, together with SML's abstraction facilities (both of which we will consider in more detail in the following chapters), make it an ideal functional language for exploring data abstraction.

Another reason for choosing SML was because of the availability of a high quality public domain compiler (Standard ML of New Jersey). The compiler is incremental, giving the benefits of a rapid interactive system with very good performance.

SML is a strongly typed language, and this was another factor in the decision. The type system which is used by strongly typed functional languages is discussed in more detail in the following section.

TYPE SYSTEMS

Strongly typed functional languages are those which incorporate type checking systems such that all functions are required to be type correct: each function is defined to operate on objects of a specified type, and application of the function to an object of inappropriate type is flagged as an error. Many functional languages are strongly typed with static type checking systems (that is, type checking is done at compile time). Examples of such languages include Hope (Burstall *et al* 1980), SML (Milner *et al* 1990) and Miranda[1] (Turner 1985a), all of which exhibit *implicit parametric* polymorphism. Briefly, *parametric* polymorphism means that a function can take parameters of many different types (provided that expressions involving the function remain well-typed). A type-checking system is said to be *implicit* if there is no need to pass types explicitly to functions. (Whenever the term polymorphism is used in this book, it can be taken as an abbreviation for implicit parametric polymorphism.) Examples of polymorphic functions will be given throughout the text. The strong, static, polymorphic type systems used by many functional languages help to prevent a lot of common programming errors and facilitate program design and implementation (Kaes 1988). Such type systems are sometimes referred to as *Hindley–Milner* systems, as the first algorithm was given by Hindley (1969) for the lambda calculus, and was independently devised by Milner (1978).

The terms *polymorphism* and *genericity* are sometimes used interchangeably, but we may need to distinguish between them, and so we give the definitions below:

- The term *polymorphism* (which is usually applied to functions) refers to the ability of a function to take parameters of different types. These parameters can be instantiated at run-time.
- The term *genericity* (which is usually applied to modules) refers to the ability of a module to take parameters of different types at compile-time. Code is then generated which depends on the particular instantiated type.

The production of generic software will be explained in more detail in Chapter 3, where we show how SML facilitates the production of generic ADTs, through the use of parametrised modules (functors).

Both polymorphism and genericity facilitate the production of reusable software components, and will be used frequently in this book.

Types in SML

The basic types of SML include `int`, `real`, `bool` and `string`. Characters are considered to be strings of length one. Compound types (such as tuples, lists and records) can be constructed by using basic and user-defined types. Types are indicated by using a single colon, and are automatically returned by the system when a type-correct expression is entered. Table 1.1 shows some examples of compound types.

Table 1.1

Compound type	Example
Tuples	`(4, "a") : int * string`
Records	`{name = "jane", age =21}: {age:int, name:string}`
Lists	`[1, 2, 3] : int list`

As explained above, the Hindley–Milner system is implicit, which means that type information can be omitted from function definitions. However, there is a limit to the

---

1 Miranda is a trademark of Research Software Ltd.

information which can be deduced by the compiler, and sometimes it is necessary to supply the type of a function's parameters to resolve possible ambiguities. In particular, this is often necessary for numerical functions, as the system may be unable to determine whether the function takes an integer or a real parameter. For example, suppose we define a function which doubles its parameter:

```
fun double n = 2*n
```

This is not a well-typed definition, as the system will be unable to deduce the type of the parameter n. The problem can be resolved by adding the type of the parameter to the definition:

```
fun double (n:int) = 2*n

>val double = fn : int -> int
```

The second line indicates the response from the system: it shows that the function double takes an integer as a parameter and returns an integer as its result.

Because functional languages are referentially transparent, the operational semantics of functions can be investigated by reducing an instantiated call to the function to normal form. The following section explains this concept (which we will use frequently) in more detail.

REDUCTION TO NORMAL FORM

An expression in a functional language can be evaluated by repeatedly rewriting or *reducing* it to its simplest (or *normal*) form, at which point it represents the result of the program. Each stage during this simplification process is called a *reduction step*. We will use the terms *reduction*, *evaluation*, *simplification* and *rewriting* to mean writing down the steps performed in a calculation. For example, suppose we reduce the expression square (3 + 4) to normal form:

```
square (3 + 4)  → square 7
                → 7 * 7
                → 49
```

An expression that can be reduced is called a *redex*, which is short for *reducible expression*. Note that if an expression has a normal form then we will always reach the same normal form, no matter what order the expression is reduced in. This is a corollary of the *Church–Rosser* theorem (Barendregt 1984). So, for example, the evaluation of square (3 + 4) could also be performed by applying the function before evaluating its parameters:

```
square (3 + 4)  → (3 + 4) * (3 + 4)
                → 7 * (3 + 4)
                → 7 * 7
                → 49
```

Throughout the text we will frequently reduce an arbitrary call to a function to verify the operational semantics of the function.

The theoretical efficiency of a function can be analysed using *asymptotic analysis*, a technique that is frequently used in mathematics, science and engineering, and which is discussed more fully in the following section.

ASYMPTOTIC ANALYSIS

At times, we may need to consider the theoretical efficiency of a function. If a function takes a parameter which is potentially infinite in size, we may be concerned about the behaviour of the function as the size of the parameter increases. Analysing the performance of a function in this way is called *asymptotic analysis*. A common method used to give an estimate of a function's efficiency is called *order* notation, a formal definition of which is given below:

- A function g with formal parameter n is said to be $O(f(n))$ if there exists a constant c such that

$$| g(n) | \leq c | f(n) |$$

for all but some finite (possibly empty) set of non-negative values for n.

A function which is $O(n)$ for some integer n is said to be *of order n*.

This notation is also referred to as *Big O* notation. It gives us an approximation of size as n tends to infinity. When programming with functional languages, the cost of evaluating a function is often taken as the number of reduction steps which are needed to reduce the expression to normal form, as this is directly proportional to the time needed to perform the computation. Using order notation we can give an approximation for the number of reduction steps that a function requires.

SUMMARY

- A *data type* (or *type*) is a means by which we can classify objects which have identical properties. A data type can be either intrinsic or user-defined.
- An *abstract data type* consists of a data type together with a set of operations, called *access functions,* which define how the type may be manipulated.
- A *data structure* or *structured data type* is an organised collection of data elements.
- *Data abstraction* refers to the use of ADTs to control the interaction between a program and its data structures.
  The advantages of using data abstraction include the following:
  - the code produced is well modularised and has high reuse potential
  - a reduction in the complexity of the software
  - the independence of the implementation is assured
  - the provision of a specification
- *Strongly typed* languages are those which incorporate type checking systems such that all functions are required to be type correct: each function is defined to operate on objects of a specified type, and application of the function to an object of inappropriate type is flagged as an error.

- An *algebraic specification* consists of two parts: the syntax of the access functions and their semantics. The latter is given by a set of axioms which define the relationship between access functions.
- Two of the advantages of using functional languages are:
  - There is a close relationship between the specification of a function and its implementation.
  - The semantics of functional programs are well-defined.

  The interchangeability of two expressions which have the same meaning is called *referential transparency*.
- The term *polymorphism* (which is usually applied to functions) refers to the ability of a function to take parameters of different types. These parameters can be instantiated at run-time.
- The term *genericity* (which is usually applied to modules) refers to the ability of a module to take parameters of different types at compile-time. Code is then generated which depends on the particular instantiated type.
- An expression can be evaluated by reducing it to its simplest (or *normal*) form. If an expression has a normal form then we will always reach the same normal form, no matter what order the expression is reduced in.
- Asymptotic analysis involves analysing the behaviour of a function as one of its parameters tends to infinity.

CHAPTER 2

Lists

INTRODUCTION

This chapter is the only one in the book which does not demonstrate an implementation of its ADT. This is simply because lists are predefined in functional languages, and are usually not considered to be abstract. Consequently, although we show how to specify the ADT list, we then go on to describe the development of some higher order functions using predefined lists and pattern matching in the usual way. We also demonstrate the development of a variety of sorting algorithms, and finish with some text processing examples which show how functional languages facilitate reuse.

DEFINITION

The ADT list is a linear sequence of an arbitrary number of items of the same type together with a number of access functions.

The list is one of the most fundamental ADTs; so fundamental, in fact, that it is provided as an intrinsic data structure in functional languages. Lists provide us with a way to collect together a group of items which all have the same type, and give us the ability to access the items linearly.

REPRESENTATION AND NOTATION

There are several ways that we can represent lists. To emphasise that we are discussing lists as ADTs in this part of the chapter we will represent them by delimiting them with round brackets, rather than the square ones which are used by most functional languages. The elements of the list are separated by commas. For example:

```
A list of integers:  (1, 9, 3, 2, 7, 8, 0)
A list of strings:   ("Sue", "Pam", "Jill")
```

etc.

(We will compare this representation with that used by SML later in the chapter.)

By convention the first item in a list is referred to as the *head* of the list. We will assume that this is the leftmost item; for example, the item at the head of the list of names ("Sue", "Pam", "Jill") is "Sue". Removing the head of a list leaves us with a list which is called the *tail* of the list. So the tail of the list of names: ("Sue", "Pam", "Jill") is the list ("Pam", "Jill").

ALGEBRAIC SPECIFICATION

In order to understand how we can manipulate the ADT list we will present an algebraic specification for it. As mentioned earlier, the type list is a predefined type in SML, but in the section that follows we will suppose that this is not the case. After presenting a possible algebraic specification we will then compare the facilities which are provided in SML for manipulating lists with the access functions which we describe below.

As explained in Chapter 1, the algebraic specification of an ADT consists of two parts: the syntax of the access functions, which gives their names, parameters and result types, and their semantics, which consists of a list of axioms specifying the relationships between them.

For generality, we will assume throughout the book that a type called item has been declared, and this will usually be used as the type of the objects in our ADTs. The aim of doing this is to facilitate the production of generic software, by ensuring that the ADTs are not dependent on the type of the objects which they hold.

Syntax of the Access Functions

The access functions for the ADT list can be split into three groups: *constructor* functions, which are so called because they are used to construct or create the data type, *predicate* functions, which are boolean valued functions used to test the data type, and *selector* functions, which select different parts of the type. We suppose in what follows that we are creating a signature for the ADT list by listing the types of its access functions; this is merely for the purpose of demonstration, and to ensure consistency with the following chapters; it is not actually possible to redefine the built-in list data structure without using a different name for the type.

There are five access functions for the ADT list from which all other functions can be built.

1. Constructor functions

There are two constructor functions, the first of which creates an empty list.

```
val empty : list
(*Post: returns an empty list *)
```

This function returns a list which does not contain any data items. The function name is preceded by the reserved word val in order to make the function heading a syntactically correct part of an SML signature.

We will use the convention of annotating each function with *pre-* and *postconditions* (abbreviated to *pre* and *post*) which state the conditions which hold before and after a function's execution respectively. Often the precondition merely states the type of the function's parameters, and so can be omitted for brevity.

The other constructor function takes two parameters, an object and a list, and constructs a new list with the object at its head and the list parameter as its tail. This function is called cons, which is short for 'construct'. For example, the result of cons ("Amy", ("Sue", "Pam", "Jill")) is the list ("Amy", "Sue", "Pam", "Jill"). If the object has type item then the signature of the function will be:

```
val cons : item -> list -> list
(*Post: returns a list with the given item as its head *)
```

2. Predicate functions

There is only one predicate function which we will need: as it is an error to try to find the head or tail of an empty list we need a predicate function to determine whether a list is empty.

```
val isempty : list -> bool
(*Post: returns true if the list is empty, otherwise false *)
```

3. Selector functions

There are two selector functions which we need, the function head:

```
val head : list -> item
(*Post: returns the item at the head of  list  *)
```

and the function tail, which returns the list which results from removing the object at the head of the list:

```
val tail: list -> list
(*Post: returns the tail of list   *)
```

Now that we have given the syntax of the access functions, we can complete the algebraic specification by giving their semantics.

Semantics of the Access Functions

The semantics of the access functions are specified by considering the behaviour of the predicate and selector functions for each possible constructor function. This method of specification is also called *case analysis*. The access functions for the ADT list must satisfy the following axioms, where x is of type item and xs is of type list:

```
1.  isempty empty  = true
2.  isempty (cons x xs) = false
3.  head empty  = error
```

```
4.  head (cons x xs) =  x
5.  tail empty = error
6.  tail (cons x xs) = xs
```

In addition, a result which is an error should result in the termination of the program's execution.

Consistency and Completeness

We must ensure that the axioms are both *consistent* and *sufficiently complete*. The definitions of these terms, which are given below, are due to Guttag (1977, 1978).

Definition

If any two axioms are contradictory then the specification is said to be *inconsistent*.

Consistency is relatively straightforward to determine by inspection, as the axioms are formulated according to our intuitive understanding of the ADT which is under discussion.

To prove that the axioms are sufficiently complete we must show that every access function has a predictable outcome for any given list. This is stated more formally by the following definition:

Definition

If the behaviour of the ADT is undefined in any situation then the axioms are said to be not *sufficiently complete*.

If the axioms are not sufficiently complete then it may be impossible to determine the behaviour of some program which uses the ADT. It can be difficult to ascertain whether or not a set of axioms satisfies this second criterion. Indeed, in Guttag (1978) there is a statement to the effect that 'in the general case the sufficient-completeness problem is unsolvable, i.e. there cannot exist a decision procedure for recognising sufficient-completeness'. However, the paper does go on to give a set of conditions that are sufficient to guarantee that an axiom set is sufficiently-complete.

Considering the given list specification, the behaviour of the constructor functions empty and cons is fully described by the syntactic part of the specification.The behaviour of isempty is given by axioms (1) and (2). The behaviour of head is given by axioms (3) and (4). The behaviour of tail is given by axioms (5) and (6).

SML is a *strict* language, which means that the values of a function's arguments are fully evaluated before the function is called. (This is in contrast with many other functional languages, such as Miranda and Haskell, which are non-strict (or *lazy*), which means that a function's arguments are only evaluated when they are required.) Because SML is strict, if a function is passed an error as an argument then we can expect it to return an error as a result. So, for example:

```
isempty (error) = error
```

Hence, our definition of a list is both consistent and sufficiently complete.

LISTS IN SML

As we mentioned at the beginning of the chapter, lists are provided as an intrinsic data structure in functional languages. We now compare the list ADT specified above with the list data structure which is provided by SML.

Representation and Notation

In SML, lists are denoted by square brackets, with the elements of the list separated by commas. For example:

```
> [9,3,1,6,7,2,3] : int list
```

Just as the ADT specified earlier has two constructor functions, so do lists in SML. To create an empty list we use square brackets, [], and to insert a value into a list we use the function :: (which is pronounced *cons*). For example:

```
1 ::  []  =  [1]

1 :: 2 :: [3,4]  = [1, 2, 3, 4]
```

The same selector functions are also provided as part of the language: to find the head of a list we can use the function hd:

```
hd  (x :: xs)  =  x
```

and to access the tail of a list we have the function tl:

```
tl  (x :: xs)  =  xs
```

However, one of the main differences between the ADT and the data structure is that we can *pattern match* against the built-in data structure. This enables us to write function definitions easily and elegantly, and means that the selector functions are unnecessary (they are merely provided for flexibility). Pattern matching also makes the predicate function isempty redundant. For example, suppose that we want to write a function double which takes a list of integers and returns a list in which the value of each of the elements has been doubled. For instance:

```
double [4,5,6,7] = [8,10,12,14]
```

We can derive the function by using case analysis. If the list is empty there is nothing to do:

```
double [] = []
```

otherwise we must double the value of the object at the head of the list and then cons this on to the tail of the list, each element of which must also be doubled :

```
double (x::xs) = 2*x::(double xs)
```

To turn this into an executable SML function, we only have to add the necessary syntactic constructs and some type information to assist the compiler, giving the function below:

```
(*Pre: takes a list of integers *)
(*Post: returns a list in which each value has been doubled *)
fun double [] = []
  | double ((x:int)::xs) = 2*x::(double xs)
```

We can compare this with the way the function would be written using the ADT:

```
fun double xs : int list = if isempty xs then empty
                           else
                           cons 2*(head xs) (double (tail xs))
```

The first version is shorter than the second, and illustrates the archetypical style in which programs are written using pattern matching in functional languages. However, for those who are not used to programming in functional languages the second version may appear to be clearer than the first.

The following section discusses the development of higher-order functions using pre-defined lists and pattern matching. It is included as an introduction for readers who are not very familiar with program development in functional languages.

HIGHER ORDER FUNCTIONS

The Function map

Suppose that we need a function which will triple every element in a list. Clearly, the design of the function will be very similar to that of the function double, the only difference being the function which is applied to each element. Similarly, if we needed a function to square every element in a list, we would also use a function with a very similar design. There are several list processing functions like these which all have the same basic pattern. Knowing this, we can abstract a new, more general function which takes a function of one argument as a parameter together with a list and returns the list in which the function has been applied to each element in the list. (We will refer to functions which take one, two or three arguments as *monadic, dyadic* and *triadic* functions, respectively.) A function which takes a function as a parameter (and possibly also returns one as its result) is called a *higher order function*. Such functions are a very powerful feature of functional languages.

We require a function which applies or maps a given function across a given list. We can develop the function (which is usually called map) by using case analysis.

If the list is empty, there is nothing to do:

```
map  f  []  =  []
```

Otherwise, we must take the head of the list, apply the function f to it, and also do this to each element in the tail of the list by calling map recursively with the tail of the list. To reconstruct the list we use :: , which gives us the second case:

```
map  f  (x::xs)  =  f x  ::  map  f  xs
```

Note that brackets are not needed on the right hand side of this equation, because functions are applied by using a space, function application associates to the left, and binds more tightly than any other operator. Thus, the definition above is equivalent to the following:

```
map  f  (x::xs)  =  (f x)  ::  (map  f  xs)
```

Adding the necessary syntactic constructs and some comments, the function can be written in SML as shown below:

```
(*Pre: takes a monadic function and a list *)
(*Post: returns a list in which the function has been applied to each
   item *)
fun map f  []  =  []
  | map f  (x::xs)  =  f x  ::  map  f  xs
```

Because of its general applicability, the function map is usually provided as part of the standard environment of functional languages, as it is in SML.

We can use this function to double every element of a list, using the function below, times2:

```
fun times2 n = 2*n
```

For example:

```
map times2 [1,2,3,4] = [2,4,6,8] : int list
```

However the need to define a function which multiplies integers by two is slightly inconvenient; we would prefer to use the built-in multiplication operator, *, if at all possible. (This will save us having to define other new functions such as times3, and so on.) We can do this by abstracting the operator away from the function, using a function ap (short for apply) which takes an operator and two arguments and applies the operator to them:

```
fun ap f x y = f (x,y)
```

In SML, an infix operator, such as *, can be made to act as a prefix operator by preceding it with the keyword op. In order to use the function ap as a parameter of higher order functions, we need to be able to apply it partially, to just one of its arguments. Using a function in this way is called currying, after H.B. Curry (Curry and Feys 1958). As an illustration of currying in action, consider the function below:

```
fun add  (x:int)  y  =  x  +  y
```

Now,
```
          add 1
```
and
```
          add 2
```

and

        add 999

are all functions of type (int → int), which means that, given one more integer, they will return an integer. Thus, the type of the function add is:

    int → (int → int)

The use of ap is similar to the use of *sections* in pure functional languages such as Miranda (Bird and Wadler 1988). Sections allow operators such as + to be treated as prefix functions by enclosing them within brackets. The operators can then take their arguments one at a time.

We can now double every element of a list by using the function ap, as shown below:

    map (ap op* 2) [2,7,8,3,5] = [4,14,16,6,10]

and similarly we can increment every element in a list:

    map (ap op+ 1) [7,4,1,7,9] = [8,5,2,8,10]

and so on.

The Function fold

Now suppose that we want to sum all the items in a list. The function is simple to write; take the head of the list and add it to the sum of the items in the tail of the list. Again, the only problem with this solution is that it is too specific. We really need to use a higher order function, so that we could also (for example) easily obtain the product of the items, or the length of the list. This functionality can be expressed by a higher order function which folds the elements in the list to produce a single result (hence the name fold). fold takes a dyadic function f, a base case b and a list and applies the function to the value b and the values in the list. There are two versions, foldr, which folds to the right, so that the function f is applied first to the last item in the list and the base case:

    foldr f b $[x_1, x_2, \ldots, x_n]$ = f x_1 (f x_2 (... (f x_n b) ...))

and foldl, which folds to the left, so that f is applied first to the head of the list and the base case:

    foldl f b $[x_1, x_2, \ldots, x_n]$ = (f ... (f (f x_1 b) x2) ... x_n)

In a strict language such as SML there is usually little to choose between foldr and foldl if the dyadic function is associative. However, it may be that one version is more efficient than the other; for example, if we concatenate a list of lists together using foldl and @ (append), then the first argument of @ will grow each time another list is folded in, whereas with foldr, the first argument stays the same length as the computation proceeds. As the efficiency of @ is proportional to the length of its first argument, this may be significant.

We will derive the definition of the function `foldr` by case analysis. If the list is empty, we return the base case:

```
foldr f b [] = b
```

Otherwise we apply the function to the head of the list and the result obtained by calling `foldr` recursively with the tail of the list:

```
foldr f b (x::xs) = f x (foldr f b xs)
```

The entire function is given below:

```
(*Pre: takes a dyadic function, a base case and a list
  Post: returns the result of applying the function to the items in
   the list and the base case *)
fun foldr f b [] = b
  | foldr f b (x::xs) = f x (foldr f b xs)
```

Now we can define functions which use `foldr`. For example:

```
(*Post: returns the sum of a list of integers *)
fun sum xs = foldr (ap op+ )   0 xs
```

and:

```
(*Post: returns the product of a list of integers *)
fun product xs = foldr (ap op* ) 1 xs
```

We have constructed a library of generally applicable functions (such as `foldr`) which are not supplied as part of the SML environment (see Appendix 1). The library is in the form of a structure (a collection of functions whose scope cannot extend that of the defining structure). Functions declared within a structure can be used either by *opening* the structure or by prefixing the function name by the name of the structure followed by a dot. For example, to access the `foldr` function, which is declared within a structure called `Library`, we can use the expression:

```
Library.foldr
```

Alternatively, the statement:

```
open Library;
```

makes all of the functions declared within the structure accessible.

EXERCISES 2.1

1. Rewrite the following expression to its simplest form, showing all working:

```
map  (ap op+ 1) [5,4,7,9]
```

2. Rewrite the following expression to its simplest form, showing all working:

```
foldr  (ap op+) 0 [1,2,3,4]
```

3. Derive the function `foldl`, (a) by using case analysis, as shown above, and (b) by using an accumulating parameter.

Continuing our introduction into the use of lists in functional languages, the next section investigates the use of lists for sorting.

SORTING

Suppose we wish to sort a set of integers into increasing order. There are a number of ways that we can proceed: the methods described below can all be categorised as *comparison* sorts, in that they operate by comparing two items (taken from the set) at a time. We will use lists to simulate sets throughout this section, and provide pseudocode specifications for each function before considering possible implementations. The efficiency of the functions will also be considered. It has been shown (Knuth 1973) that the lower bound for the complexity of any comparison sort of n items is $O(n\log_2 n)$.

Bubble Sort

The *bubble* sort is so called because items to be sorted gradually bubble towards their correct position. Another name for this sort is *exchange* sort, because of the way that items are exchanged until the set is sorted.

Suppose we have n integers stored in a list which is indexed from zero. The bubble sort algorithm can be pseudocoded as shown below:

```
fun bubblesort
(*Post: returns a sorted list of integers *)

for all i from 0 to (n-1) do
    compare items i and i+1
    swop the items so that the smallest is nearest to the head of the
      list
until the list is sorted
```

For example, consider using bubble sort to sort the list of nine integers shown below. The first pass through the list proceeds as follows:

```
bubblesort [7, 1, ~5, 9, 3, 6, 4, ~2, 8]      compare items 0 and 1 and
                                                 swop them
  → bubblesort [1, 7, ~5, 9, 3, 6, 4, ~2, 8]   compare items 1 and 2 and
                                                 swop them
  → bubblesort [1, ~5, 7, 9, 3, 6, 4, ~2, 8]   compare items 2 and 3
  → bubblesort [1, ~5, 7, 9, 3, 6, 4, ~2, 8]   compare items 3 and 4 and
                                                 swop them
  → bubblesort [1, ~5, 7, 3, 9, 6, 4, ~2, 8]   compare items 4 and 5 and
                                                 swop them
```

```
→ bubblesort [1, ~5, 7, 3, 6, 9, 4, ~2, 8]    compare items 5 and 6 and
                                               swop them
→ bubblesort [1, ~5, 7, 3, 6, 4, 9, ~2, 8]    compare items 6 and 7 and
                                               swop them
→ bubblesort [1, ~5, 7, 3, 6, 4, ~2, 9, 8]    compare items 7 and 8 and
                                               swop them
→ bubblesort [1, ~5, 7, 3, 6, 4, ~2, 8, 9]
```

(Note: ~ denotes unary minus in SML.)

At the end of the first pass through the list, the largest item is stored in the correct position. Now the process must be repeated, so that the next largest item is stored in the correct position, and so on until the list is sorted. The results for each pass through the above list are shown below:

```
2nd pass:            [~5, 1, 3, 6, 4, ~2, 7, 8, 9]
3rd pass:            [~5, 1, 3, 4, ~2, 6, 7, 8, 9]
4th pass:            [~5, 1, 3, ~2, 4, 6, 7, 8, 9]
5th pass:            [~5, 1, ~2, 3, 4, 6, 7, 8, 9]
6th (and last) pass: [~5, ~2, 1, 3, 4, 6, 7, 8, 9]
```

Asymptotic analysis

Unfortunately, bubble sort is not very efficient; analysis shows that it requires $O(n^2)$ comparisons and $O(n^2)$ exchanges, for both the average and the worst case. However, for an already sorted set of items, bubble sort requires $O(n)$ comparisons, and no exchanges.

Implementation

From the pseudocode, we can see that bubble sort operates by swopping items until the list is sorted. So we can write the top level function as:

```
fun bubblesort xs = until is_sorted swop xs
```

where `until` is an iterative function which takes a predicate function, a monadic function and an object and applies the function to the object until the predicate is satisfied. The function being applied, `swop`, compares adjacent items in a list and exchanges them if necessary. It is specific to the bubble sort algorithm, and is straightforward to implement by case analysis on an empty list, a singleton list and a list with two or more items:

```
(*Pre: takes a list of integers *)
(*Post: moves the largest item to the right *)
fun swop [] = []
  | swop [x] = [x]
  | swop (x::y::xs):int list = if x <= y then
                                   x::swop (y::xs)
                                   else y::swop (x::xs)
```

The function `until` is a general purpose function, which we have provided within our library structure (see Appendix 1). We can code it as:

```
(*Pre: takes a predicate, a monadic function and an object  *)
(*Post: applies the function to the object until the predicate is true
 *)
fun until p f x = if p x then x
                       else until p f (f x)
```

The function is_sorted takes a list and returns true if it is sorted in non-decreasing order (that is, with the smallest item at the head of the list). This function needs to compare successive items to determine whether or not the list is sorted. To achieve this, we will form a list of pairs, where the first pair consists of the first and second items in the list, the second pair consists of the second and third items in the list, and so on. The function is_sorted should return true if all of the booleans produced by comparing the items in each pair are true. So we need two auxiliary, general purpose functions: zip (to form a list of pairs from a pair of lists) and alltrue, which returns true if, after applying the predicate to the items in the list, all of the items in the resulting list are true. These are both simple to implement, again by case analysis, and are provided as part of our library of utility functions:

```
(*Pre: takes a pair of lists *)
(*Post: returns a list of pairs *)
fun   zip [] ys = []
    | zip (x::xs) [] = []
    | zip (x::xs) (y::ys) = (x,y)::zip xs ys
```

```
(*Pre: takes a predicate and a list *)
(*Post: returns true if all of the booleans produced by mapping the
  predicate over the list are true  *)
fun alltrue p [] = true
   | alltrue p (x::xs) = (p x) andalso alltrue p xs
```

Using these functions, we can produce the function is_sorted:

```
(*Pre: takes a list of integers *)
(*Post: returns true if the list is sorted *)
fun is_sorted (xs:int list):bool = let fun isless (x, (y:int)) = x<y
                                       in alltrue isless (zip xs (tl xs))
                                       end
```

This completes our implementation of bubblesort.

Quicksort

Quicksort is a divide and conquer algorithm, in that it operates by dividing the data set into two distinct parts on each iteration. A pivot is chosen at random from the set, and is used to divide the set into two parts, one consisting of the items which are less than the pivot, and another consisting of the items which are greater than the pivot. The two subsets are sorted (using quicksort) and then the results and pivot are concatenated together.

Assuming that the set of integers is stored in a list, we can pseudocode quicksort as:

```
fun qsort
(*Post: returns a sorted list of integers *)
```

```
choose an item n from the list
return (qsort(items which are ≤ n)) @ [n] @ (qsort(items which are > n))
```

(Note: @ is the *append* operator in SML; it takes two lists and returns the result of joining the two together.) For example, suppose that we rewrite a call to quicksort a list of integers using the head of the list as the pivot:

```
qsort [7, 1, ~5, 9, 3, 6, 4, ~2, 8] → qsort [1, ~5, 3, 6, 4,~2] @ [7]
                                                          @ qsort [9, 8]
```

Now,

```
qsort [1, ~5, 3, 6, 4,~2]  → qsort [~5, ~2] @ [1] @ qsort [3, 6, 4]
```

and

```
qsort [~5,~2] → qsort [] @  [~5] @ qsort [~2]
```

and

```
qsort [~2] → [~2]
```

so

```
qsort [~5,~2] → [~5,~2]
```

Similarly,

```
qsort [3, 6, 4]     → qsort [] @ [3] @ qsort [6,4]
                    → [3, 4, 6]
```

so

```
qsort [1, ~5, 3, 6, 4,~2]  →  [~5, ~2, 1,  3, 4, 6]
```

and

```
qsort [9, 8] →  [8,9]
```

so that

```
qsort [7, 1, ~5, 9, 3, 6, 4, ~2, 8] →  [~5, ~2, 1,  3, 4, 6, 7, 8, 9]
```

Asymptotic analysis

Quicksort requires $O(n\log_2 n)$ comparisons for both the average and the best case. Experimental results show that for the average case the constant is small, and, in fact, this is the best internal sorting method for such a case (Horowitz and Sahni 1976). However, in the worst case quicksort requires $O(n^2)$ comparisons.

Implementation

We can derive the implementation from the pseudocode, using case analysis. If the list is empty, then we return an empty list:

```
qsort [] = []
```

Otherwise, we choose an item from the list (the head of the list, say), and quicksort the items which are both lesser and greater than it, appending the results together:

```
qsort (x::xs) = qsort (filter (ap op>= x) xs) @ [x] @
                                    qsort (filter (ap op< x) xs)
```

where `filter` is a library function which takes a predicate function and a list and returns a list consisting of those items for which the predicate holds:

```
(*Pre: takes a predicate and a list *)
(*Post: returns a list for which the predicate holds *)
fun filter p [] = []
  | filter p (x::xs) = if p x then x::filter p xs
                       else filter p xs
```

For example, the predicate function in the first case is given by the expression (ap op>= x), which applies the function (x >=) to the integers in the list, returning the ones which x is greater than.

Putting the two cases for quicksort together and adding the necessary syntactic constructs, we arrive at the following SML function:

```
fun qsort [] = []
  | qsort (x::xs):int list = qsort (filter (ap op>= x) xs) @ [x] @
                                    qsort (filter (ap op< x) xs)
```

Insertion Sort

Insertion sort operates by inserting one element at a time into its correct position in a sorted list. Initially, the sorted list is empty; as each item is added to it, the result list is gradually accumulated. The pseudocode is shown below:

```
fun isort
(*Post: returns a sorted list of integers *)

for each item in the list do
     insert the item into its correct position into the sorted list
```

For example, the evaluation of `isort` for a list of four integers proceeds as follows:

```
isort  [7, 1, ~5, 9] →   insert 7 (isort [1, ~5, 9])
                     →   insert 7 (insert 1 (isort [~5, 9]))
                     →   insert 7 (insert 1 (insert ~5 (isort [9])))
                     →   insert 7 (insert 1 [~5, 9])
                     →   [~5, 1, 7, 9]
```

Asymptotic analysis

Insertion sort requires $O(n^2)$ comparisons and $O(n^2)$ exchanges, for both the average and the worst cases, and $O(n)$ comparisons for a set of items which is 'almost' sorted (Sedgewick 1988).

Implementation

A straightforward implementation, derived from the pseudocode using case analysis, is given below:

```
fun isort [] = []
  | isort (x::xs) = insert x (isort xs)
```

where insert is a function which ensures that each item is placed in its correct position:

```
(*Pre: takes an integer and a sorted list *)
(*Post: returns a sorted list with the integer inserted *)
fun insert (x:int) [] = [x]
  | insert x (y::ys) = if x < y then x::y::ys
                       else y::insert x ys
```

Alternatively, we could make use of some more of our library functions, and write the insertion sort as shown below:

```
fun isort []:int list = []
  | isort xs = foldr insert [] xs

fun insert (x:int) xs = (takewhile (ap op>= x ) xs) @ [x] @ (dropwhile
                                                      (ap op>= x ) xs)
```

where foldr is the function introduced earlier in the chapter, and takewhile and dropwhile are standard list manipulation functions, which are supplied in our library structure:

```
(*Pre: takes a predicate and a list *)
(*Post: returns the longest initial segment of the list for which the
  predicate holds *)
fun takewhile p [] = []
  | takewhile p (x::xs) = if p x then x::takewhile p xs
                          else []

(*Pre: takes a predicate and a list *)
(*Post: removes the longest initial segment of the list for which the
  predicate holds *)
fun dropwhile p [] = []
  | dropwhile p (x::xs) = if p x then dropwhile p xs
                          else x::xs
```

Merge Sort

Merge sort is another divide and conquer algorithm, which operates by dividing the set to be sorted into two halves, sorting each half separately (using merge sort) and then merging the two halves back together again, taking care to ensure that the order of the resulting set is still correct. A pseudocode description which assumes a list implementation is given below:

```
fun msort
(*Post: returns a sorted list of integers *)

divide the list into two
sort each half and merge the resulting lists together
```

For example, a merge sort of a list of four integers proceeds as follows:

```
msort  [7, 1, ~5, 9] →  merge (msort [7, 1]) (msort [~5, 9])
                     →  merge (merge (msort [7]) (msort [1])) (merge
                                                   (msort [~5]) (msort [9]))
                     →  merge (merge [7] [1]) (merge [~5] [9])
                     →  merge [1,7 ] [~5, 9]
                     →  [~5, 1, 7, 9]
```

Asymptotic analysis

Merge sort requires $O(n\log_2 n)$ comparisons to sort any set of n integers, whether the set is a random, sorted or inverted (i.e. reverse sorted) set of items.

Implementation

We can use the predefined function length to divide the list into two. If the list is empty or is of length one, then we return the original list. Otherwise, we can use the two standard functions, take and drop, together with a function which merges the lists together, to produce the following function:

```
fun msort xs = let val n = length xs
            in  if n <= 1 then xs
                else
                let val ys = take (n div 2) xs
                    val zs = drop (n div 2) xs
                in merge (msort ys) (msort zs)
                end
        end
```

The functions take and drop are general purpose library functions, which take and drop (respectively) *n* items from a list:

```
(*Post: drops the first n items from a list *)
fun drop 0 xs = xs
  | drop n [] = []
  | drop (n:int) (x::xs) = drop (n-1) xs

(*Post: returns the first n items of a list *)
fun take 0 xs = []
  | take n [] = []
  | take (n:int) (x::xs) = x::take (n-1) xs
```

The function merge takes two sorted lists and joins them together, maintaining the ordering of the resulting list:

```
(*Pre: takes 2 sorted lists *)
(*Post: returns 1 sorted list *)
fun merge [] ys = ys
  | merge (x::xs) [] = (x::xs)
  | merge (x::xs) (y::ys) = if (x:int) <= y then x::merge xs (y::ys)
                            else y::merge (x::xs) ys
```

Selection Sort

Selection sort operates by selecting the smallest (for a non-decreasing sort) item in a list and adding this to the front of the result of sorting the rest of the list using selection sort. The algorithm can be described by the following pseudocode:

```
fun ssort
(*Post: returns a sorted list of integers *)

for a list of items do
find the smallest item in the list
add this to the front of the result of sorting the rest of the list
```

For example, a call to selection sort a list of four random integers would proceed as follows:

```
ssort [7, 1, ~5, 9] →   ~5 :: ssort [7,1,9]
                    →   ~5 :: (1 :: ssort [7,9])
                    →   ~5 :: (1 :: (7 :: ssort [9]))
                    →   ~5 :: (1 :: (7 :: (9 :: [])))
                    →   [~5, 1, 7, 9 ]
```

Asymptotic analysis

Selection sort requires $O(n^2)$ comparisons to sort any set of n integers, whether the set is a random, sorted or inverted set of items, for the implementation shown here. (Later, we will discuss a more efficient implementation, called heap sort, which uses a tree and has $O(n\log_2 n)$ complexity.)

Implementation

Selection sort is straightforward to implement:

```
fun ssort [] = []
  | ssort xs = let val x = min xs
               in x::ssort (xs--[x])
               end
```

where -- is an infix list difference function, supplied in our library, which returns the result of subtracting one list from another:

```
infix --
(*Post: returns the items in the first list which are not in the
   second *)
fun xs -- [] = xs
  | xs -- (y::ys) = let fun remove [] y = []
                          | remove (x::xs) y = if x = y then xs
                                               else x::(remove xs y)
                    in ((remove xs y) -- ys)
                    end
```

The function min (which is also a library function) is given below:

```
(*Post: returns the minimum of a list of integers *)
fun min xs = foldl1 min2 xs
```

where:

```
(*Post: returns the minimum of 2 integers *)
fun min2 a (b:int) = if a<=b then a
                     else b
```

This uses foldl1, a function which folds a non-empty list by taking two items at a time and applying a function to them. Note that foldl and foldl1 are very similar functions, the only differences being that the latter is not defined for empty lists and does not require a base case:

```
(*Pre: takes a non-empty list *)
(*Post: applies a dyadic function to 2 items at a time and returns the
   result *)
fun foldl1 f (x::xs) = foldl f x xs
```

where foldl is the standard function which folds a list in a left associative manner:

```
(*Post: returns the result of applying the dyadic function f to items
   in the list and the base case *)
fun foldl f a [] = a
  | foldl f a (x::xs) = foldl f (f a x) xs
```

Bucket Sort

Bucket sort can be used if the items to be sorted fall into some pre-determined domain. It operates by dividing the domain into a number of intervals, and then sorting (using insertion sort, usually) these smaller sets of items and concatenating the results. Using pseudocode and assuming a list implementation we can express the algorithm as:

```
fun bucketsort
(*Post: returns a sorted list of integers *)

for the items in a list do
filter the smallest items in some interval and sort them using
   insertion sort
```

return this sublist @ the result of bucket sorting the rest of the
   list

For example, suppose the predetermined interval is [0, 100) (that is, including 0 but
less than 100), and suppose that this interval is to be divided into ten subdomains, [0,10),
[10,20), ..., [90,100). Then an evaluation of a call to bucket sort may proceed as follows
(missing out some of the intermediate steps):

```
bucketsort  [25, 36, 14, 9, 56, 21, 55, 72, 84, 93, 6, 51, 62, 75, 37,
                                                              12, 95]

→ isort [9, 6] @ bucketsort  [25, 36, 14, 56, 21, 55, 72, 84, 93, 51,
                                                     62, 75, 37, 12, 95]
→ [6, 9] @ isort [14,12] @ bucketsort  [25, 36,  56, 21, 55, 72, 84,
                                             93, 51, 62, 75, 37, 95]
...
...
→ [6, 9] @ [12, 14] @ [21, 25] @ [36, 37] @ [51, 55, 56] @ [62] @ [72,
                                        75] @ [84] @ [93, 95]
→ [6, 9, 12, 14, 21, 25, 36, 37, 51, 55, 56, 62, 72, 75, 84, 93, 95 ]
```

Asymptotic analysis

Bucket sort requires $O(n)$ comparisons to sort a random set of n items. However, in the
worst case, bucket sort degenerates to insertion sort, and requires $O(n^2)$ comparisons.

Implementation

Assume that the items to be sorted are integers in the range [a, b). Then we can implement bucket sort as shown below:

```
fun bucketsort xs a b = let val i = a
          in let fun bsort xs j = if j< b then
                        let val ys = filter (inrange (j, j+(b div 10))) xs
                        in isort ys @ bsort (xs –– ys) (j+ (b div 10))
                        end
                                    else []
              in bsort xs i
              end
       end
```

The local function, bsort, takes the lower bound as its second parameter, and uses this
to divide the domain into intervals (in this case, of ten integers).
   The function inrange is a predicate function:

```
(*Post: returns true if x lies between a and b, otherwise false *)
fun inrange (a,b) (x:int) = x >= a andalso x < b
```

We are also reusing two of our standard library functions, the list difference function,
––, and the function filter.

Shell Sort

Shell sort, like merge sort, operates by sorting sublists (using insertion sort). However, unlike merge sort, the sublists are chosen by the positions of the items in the list. Typically, the sort would start with items separated by a distance of 13, then switch to sublists with 4 items, and finally use insertion sort for the entire list. For example, for a set of 15 items, we could start with sublists of items indexed by 0 and 13, 1 and 14, etc., and then switch to sublists of items indexed by 0, 3, 6, 9, 12, 15 and 1, 4, 7, 10, 13 and so on. It has been shown (Sedgewick, 1988) that the increment sequence (13, 4, 1) leads to an efficient sort, but other increment sequences may be more efficient. The algorithm works well, because it reduces the total number of passes which would be needed if a straight insertion sort were used. Shell sort is also known as *diminishing increment sort*.

The pseudocode for shell sort is given below.

```
fun shellsort
(*Post: returns a sorted list of integers *)

for a list of items do
     for a set of distances do
          isort sublists of items separated by the distance
```

Asymptotic analysis

The asymptotic analysis of shell sort is complicated, but empirical results indicate that it requires $O(n^{1.5})$ comparisons to sort a random set of n items, and in the worst case this degenerates to $O(n^2)$ comparisons (Sedgewick 1988).

The implementation of shell sort is left as an exercise for the reader.

The aim of the following example is to demonstrate how functional languages can be used to design reusable software, and to illustrate the role that standard library functions can play in the development of software systems.

AN EXAMPLE OF SOFTWARE REUSE

This example is a case study in text processing.

Specification

Suppose that we want to write a program which will accept a piece of text and which produces a count of the number of words in the text.

The requirements analysis is outlined in more detail below:

A piece of text is assumed to consist of sentences separated by full stops. Each sentence consists of words separated by one or more space characters (where a space character is a blank, " ", newline, "\n", or tab, "\t") and possibly other punctuation characters, and each word is a list of alphabetical characters. We will assume that the count required is the total of the number of words in the text. The punctuation characters are assumed to be given by the string:

```
punct = [ ",",",",":","(",")",";",";","'","\""]
```

and the spaces which can be ignored are given by the string:

```
blanks = ["\n","\t"]
```

(The final item in the punctuation list, \", is the escape sequence for a double quote, ".)

A possible solution to this problem involves counting the words in each sentence and then summing the counts. The design is outlined by the following pseudocode, where the function total takes a string and returns an integer:

```
fun total
(*Pre: takes a string *)
(*Post: returns the total number of words in the string *)


count the words in each sentence
sum the counts to find the total
```

This uses the function count, which takes the input text (which is in the form of a string), formats it (first into sentences and then into words) and returns a list of numbers representing the number of words in each sentence. The function can be specified using the following pseudocode:

```
fun count
(*Pre: takes a string *)
(*Post: returns a list of numbers, each of which represents the number
   of words in a sentence *)


replace punctuation and ignored spaces by blanks
remove excess blanks
split the resulting clean text into sentences
split_up the resulting sentences into words
count the words in each sentence
```

Now we must refine each of the functions referred to in the pseudocode. We start with replace, which can be refined as:

```
fun replace
(*Pre:  takes a string *)
(*Post: returns a list of strings, in which all punctuation, newlines
   and tabs are replaced by blanks *)

for the string do
     if a char is in the list of ignored punctuation or blanks then
          replace it by a blank
     otherwise do nothing
```

Note that because the function replace has to process each character separately, and characters are treated as strings of unit length in SML, replace will return a list of strings (each of which corresponds to one character).

The function replace has the effect of inserting extra blanks into the text; these may be unwanted, if (for example) the text were later to be searched for a particular phrase, in which case the blanks would be significant. Consequently, we will need the function reformat, which removes the excess spaces inserted by replace.

```
fun reformat
(*Pre:  takes a list of strings *)
(*Post: removes the extra blanks inserted by replace and returns a
  list of strings *)

for a list of strings  do
    if 2 consecutive chars are both blanks, then
          remove one of them
    otherwise do nothing
```

The function split takes the list of strings produced by reformat and splits them up into sentences. Its pseudocode is given below:

```
fun split
(*Pre:  takes a list of strings *)
(*Post: returns a list of strings, formatted as sentences *)

for a list of strings do
    if the list is empty then nothing
    if  the 1st char is a full stop or a blank then ignore it
    otherwise  sent::(split rest)
    where
    sent is a sequence of chars ending in a full stop
    rest is the rest of the text
```

To enable us to count individual words, we will use the function split_up, which takes a sentence and splits it up into words. This can be refined as:

```
fun split_up
(*Pre:  takes a string corresponding to a sentence *)
(*Post: returns a list of strings, corresponding to the words in a
  sentence *)

for a sentence do
    if it is empty then nothing
    if  the 1st char is a blank then ignore it
    otherwise  first::(split_up rest)
    where
    first is a sequence of consecutive non-blank chars
    rest is the rest of the sentence
```

The function findtotal returns the total number of words in a sentence, and can be refined as:

```
fun findtotal
(*Pre:  takes a  list of any type *)
(*Post: returns the number of items in the list (for this example, the
  number of words in a sentence) *)

for a list of words do
    ignore each word but increment a counter from 0
```

This finishes the specification of the function count. The function sum simply takes a list of integers and adds them up:

```
fun sum
(*Pre: takes a list of integers *)
(*Post: returns their sum *)
```

Having specified each of the functions which we will need, we now consider their implementation.

Implementation

The function total is a composition of two functions, count and sum. This can be implemented directly, using function composition, o:

```
fun total xs = (sum o count) xs
```

(Note: (f o g) x is equivalent to f (g x).)

The function sum takes a list of integers and returns their sum. It is of general use and so is provided within our library of standard functions. Its implementation is given below:

```
fun sum xs = foldl (ap op+) 0 xs
```

This applies the operator, +, to each of the integers in the list, using a base case of zero.

The function count can also be implemented as a composition of the specified functions, as follows:

```
fun count xs = (map findtotal o map split_up o split o reformat o
                                                        replace) xs
```

The functions used by count can be coded from the pseudocode given above. The function replace is implemented as:

```
fun replace xs = let
        fun valid c = let val punct = [",",":","(",")",";","'","\""]
                          val blanks = ["\n","\t"]
                      in
                      if c member punct orelse c member blanks then
                          " "
                      else c
                      end
        in
        map valid (explode xs)
        end
```

The function map is provided by the SML standard environment, and applies a given function to every element of a list, as discussed earlier. The function explode must be applied to the string xs to obtain a list of characters, which can then be processed individually. It is supplied as part of the Standard ML environment, and can be specified informally as follows:

```
fun explode
(*Pre: takes a string *)
(*Post: returns a list of characters *)
```

The function member is part of the library structure which we have provided to supplement the standard environment. The function is implemented as an infix function, using map and another standard function, exists, which takes a predicate function and a list, and returns true if, after applying the predicate to the items in the list, one of the items in the resulting list is true.

```
(*Pre: takes a predicate and a list *)
(*Post: returns true if one of the booleans produced by mapping the
   predicate over the list is true  *)
fun exists p [] = true
  | exists p (x::xs) = (p x) orelse exists p xs
```

Thus, member can be written as:

```
(*Post: returns true if the given item is in the given list *)
infix member
fun x member xs = exists (ap op= x) xs
```

The function reformat ensures that there is only ever one blank between words, and it is coded from the pseudocode, using case analysis on the list, as shown below:

```
fun reformat (c::d::cs) = if  c = " " andalso d = " " then
                            reformat (d::cs)
                          else
                            (c::reformat (d::cs))
  | reformat [c] = if c = " " then []
                   else [c]
  | reformat [] = []
```

The function split, which splits a string into sentences, can be implemented as follows:

```
fun split [] = []
  | split (".")::cs) = split cs
  | split (" "::cs)  = split cs          (*only applies if " " occurs
                                              between sentences*)
  | split cs = let
                 val sent = takewhile (ap op<> ".") cs
                 val rest = dropwhile (ap op<> ".") cs
               in
               ((implode sent)::(split rest))
               end
```

Note the use of the function implode here, a function provided as part of the standard environment, which takes a list of strings (the individual characters) and turns them into a single string corresponding to a sentence:

```
fun implode
(*Pre: takes a list of strings *)
(*Post: returns the result of concatenating the strings together *)
```

Thus, `implode` is the inverse of `explode`.

The functions `takewhile` and `dropwhile` are also provided by our library (their implementation was given earlier in the chapter). The former, applied to a predicate and a list, takes elements from the front of the list while the predicate is satisfied, whereas the latter, applied to a predicate and a list, removes elements from the front of the list while the predicate is satisfied.

The function `split-up` can be implemented in a similar manner to `split`, using an auxiliary function, `split_up'`, which treats the characters individually (hence the use of `explode` within the function `split_up`).

```
fun split_up' []  = []
  | split_up' (" "::cs) = split_up' cs
  | split_up' cs  = let
                        val word = takewhile (ap op<>" ") cs
                        val rest = dropwhile (ap op<>" ") cs
                    in
                        (implode word)::(split_up' rest)
                    end

fun split_up cs = split_up' (explode cs)
```

Finally, the function `findtotal` can be implemented as:

```
fun findtotal xs = let fun inc w n = n+1
                   in
                   foldr inc 0 xs
                   end
```

This makes use of the function `foldr`, which is part of our library structure, and which folds up a list in a right associative manner.

The functions were implemented and tested using an incremental bottom-up strategy (Boehm *et al* 1984) as exemplified in the next section.

Validation

We can now validate the software incrementally, so that every function is tested before it is incorporated into the system.

We can perform black-box testing for the function `replace`, by calling the function with different input data, as shown below:

```
implode (replace "a,b.")
> "a b." : string
```

where lines marked with an arrow, >, indicate the response from the SML system. The use of `implode` here is merely to make the output more readable, as `replace` returns a list of strings. We can test various inputs, paying attention to special cases such as empty lists, and lists of punctuation characters:

```
implode (replace "")
>"" : string
```

```
implode (replace ",:();\'\"")
> "        " : string

implode (replace "a\nb,c.d:e(f)g;h")
>"a b c.d e f g h" : string
```

If we want to test replace by taking the input data from a file and writing the output to a file, then it will be necessary to use SML's input and output primitives. For input, the functions open_in and input, which have the following signatures, are provided. (In SML, the reserved word val is used to introduce a function's signature (i.e. its type).)

```
val open_in :  string →  instream
(*Post : returns a stream connected to the given file *)

val input :  instream * int →  string
(*Post: returns the first n chars of the given file, where n is
   supplied as the 2nd parameter *)
```

Similarly, for output, we will use the functions open_out and output:

```
val open_out :  string →  outstream
(*Post : returns a stream connected to the given file *)

val output :  outstream * string →  unit
(*Post: writes the string to the given file *)
```

We will incorporate these functions into a function called format, which will also call the function implode:

```
val format : string →  string list →  unit
(*Pre: takes a filename and a list of strings *)
(*Post: opens the named file and outputs the concatenated list of
   strings to it *)

fun format f xs = output (open_out f, implode xs)
```

For example, to take a string of 1000 characters from a file called data, and send the result returned by replace to another file called f, we could use an expression of the form:

```
format "f" ((replace (input ((open_in "data"), 1000))))
```

In order to perform further testing with replace, we first black-box test the function member and also implement a testing function, validchars:

```
fun validchars [] = true
  | validchars (x::xs) = let val punct = [",",":",":","(",")",";","'","\""]
                             val blanks = ["\n","\t"]
                         in
                         (alltrue (not_in blanks) xs) andalso (alltrue
                                                      (not_in punct) xs)
                         end
```

where

```
fun not_in [] x = true
  | not_in xs x = not (x member xs)
```

and `alltrue` is our library function which returns true if, after applying a predicate function to a list, all of the results are true.

After testing this function, it can be used to validate the function `replace`:

```
validchars (replace "a\nb,c.d:e(f)g;h")
>true : bool
```

etc.

The function reformat can be validated in a similar manner.

We can perform isolated black-box testing on the functions `split` and `split_up`:

```
split (explode "The theory. Of types")
> ["The theory","Of types"] : string list
```

(Note the use of `explode` here, which is due to the fact that `split` takes a list of strings.)

```
split_up ( "The theory of types")
> ["The","theory","of","types"] : string list
```

and we can also integrate the functions `replace`, `reformat`, `split` and `split_up`, and test the result with input from a file. For example, using the file `data`, which contains the string:

```
One of the main problems that is central to
    the software production
process is to identify the nature of "progress"
    and to find some way of
measuring it. There is no theory which enables
us to calculate limits
on the size, performance or complexity of software.
```

(Fraser 1969, David 1969) with the following expression:

```
(map split_up (split (reformat (replace (input ((open_in "data"), 1000
                                                                )))))))
```

produces the result:

```
>[["One","of","the","main","problems","that","is","central","to",
"the","software","production",...], ["There","is","no","theory",
"which","enables","us","to","calculate","limits","on","the",...]] :
string list list
```

This illustrates the necessity of sending output to a file; after a certain point the SML compiler abbreviates the output to three dots.

We can perform isolated black-box testing on the function `findtotal`. For example:

```
findtotal ["The", "theory", "of", "types"];
> 4 : int
```

and so on. Finally, we can also perform integration testing on various sets of input data. For example, using the file called data which we had earlier, and an empty file called empty:

```
total (input ((open_in "data"), 1000));
> 46 : int

total (input ((open_in "empty"),1000));
> 0 : int
```

The advantage of performing such dynamic testing in conjunction with software development is that any design errors can be located immediately and remedied.

Modifying the Specification

We now consider the ease with which the prototype can be reused to accommodate modifications in the initial specification. This is a crucial part of the software development process: software which has been designed to facilitate reuse helps to minimise the cost of maintenance and the cost of re-engineering. Let us suppose that the customer for whom the software was written, on reading the informal specification given earlier (or on using the software), realises that it is incorrect: the count which was required was actually the number of occurrences of each individual word, rather than the total number of words in the text. The customer also stipulates at this point that the program must sort the resulting word counts alphabetically. This necessitates revising our specification and implementation to satisfy these requirements. Luckily, this is not difficult, as we show in the following sections.

Specification

By analysing the customer's requirements, we can formulate the following, modified, informal specification:

Write a program which will accept a piece of text and produce a sorted list of words and numbers, where the numbers represent the frequency of occurrence of each word. The text is assumed to be formatted as previously specified. The output must be sorted alphabetically. We assume that upper case letters precede lower case in this solution.

The top-level function, sort_and_count, will call a function to add a count to each word in a sentence, and will then concatenate the results for each sentence and call a sorting function followed by a function which sums the frequency counts:

```
fun sort_and_count
(*Pre: takes a string *)
(*Post: returns a list of (string, int) pairs, each of which
  represents a word and its associated frequency *)
```

```
add a count to each word, using count_each
concatenate the results using concat
sort the (word, freq) list using wordsort
sum the frequencies using freq_count
```

The pseudocode for the function count_each, is given below:

```
fun count_each
(*Pre: takes a string *)
(*Post: returns a list of lists of (word, freq) pairs, where each list
  corresponds to a sentence *)

replace punctuation and ignored spaces by blanks
remove excess blanks
split the resulting clean text into sentences
split_up the resulting sentences into words
add a count to each word in a sentence using countwords
```

This uses four of the functions that we implemented for the previous system, and one new function, countwords, which can be specified as follows:

```
fun countwords
(*Pre: takes a list of words (corresponding to a sentence) *)
(*Post: returns the list with an integer associated with each word *)

for a list of words do
    form a list of (word, freq) pairs
    where freq is 1 for the 1st occurrence of word,
      or is incremented by 1 otherwise
```

The function concat which is used by sort_and_count is supplied as part of our library, and is used to rejoin the list of lists of pairs into a single list of pairs. The function wordsort can be specified as shown below:

```
fun wordsort
(*Pre: takes a list of (word, freq) pairs *)
(*Post: returns a sorted list of pairs *)

for a list of pairs do
    sort the list
```

After sorting the list, any words which are identical will be in consecutive positions in the list, allowing us to design the function freq_count as follows:

```
fun freq_count
(*Pre: takes a list of (item, int) pairs *)
(*Post: returns a list of (item, int) pairs without duplicates, where
  the int represents the items' frequency of occurrence*)

for a sorted list of (word, freq) pairs do
    increment freq by 1 if 2 successive words are the same
    otherwise inspect the next 2 pairs
```

We now turn to the implementation of the additional functions.

Implementation

The implementation is straightforward: function composition can be used to implement
the functions sort_and_count and count_each:

```
fun sort_and_count xs = (freq_count o wordsort o concat o count_each)
                                                                    xs
```

```
fun count_each ws = (map countwords o map split_up o split o reformat
                                                           o replace) ws
```

We use the function foldr to implement countwords:

```
fun countwords ws = let
              fun update w [] = [(w,1)]
                | update w ((x,n)::wcs) = if w=x then (w,n+1)::wcs
                                          else
                                              (x,n)::(update w wcs)
              in
              foldr update [] ws
              end
```

The function wordsort can be implemented by adapting our quicksort function to take
a list of pairs:

```
fun wordsort [] = []
  | wordsort (x::xs):(string * int) list = wordsort (filter (ismore x)
                            xs)@ [x]@wordsort (filter (isless x) xs)
```

where:

```
(*Post: returns true if the first word succeeds the second *)
fun ismore (w1:string,c1) (w2,c2) = w1 >= w2
```

and:

```
(*Post: returns true if the first word precedes the second *)
fun isless (w1:string,c1) (w2,c2) = w1 < w2
```

The function freq_count is also straightforward to implement:

```
fun freq_count ((w1,c1:int)::(w2,c2)::ws)
                    = if w1=w2 then freq_count ((w1,c1+c2)::ws)
                      else (w1,c1)::freq_count ((w2,c2)::ws)
  | freq_count [(w,c)] = [(w,c)]
  | freq_count [] = []
```

The modifications have been accomplished with a high degree of software reuse and a
minimum number of changes. The software can now be validated dynamically, as shown
in the following section.

Validation

The function countwords can be validated using expressions of the form:

```
countwords ["The","theory","of","types"];
> [("types",1),("of",1),("theory",1),("The",1)] : (string * int) list
```

As we have already validated the functions replace, reformat, split and split_up, this completes the testing of the functions which constitute the count_each. To validate the result of integrating the functions, we can use expressions of the form shown below:

```
count_each (input ((open_in "empty"), 1000));
> [] : (string * int) list list
```

```
count_each (input ((open_in "data"), 1000));
>[[("it",1),("measuring",1),("of",3),("way",1),("some",1),("find",1),
  ("to",3),("and",1),("progress",1),("nature",1),("the",3),("identify",
         1),...],[("software",1),("of",1),("complexity",1),("or",1),
           ("performance",1),("size",1),("the",1),("on",1),("limits",1),
         ("calculate",1),("to",1),("us",1),...]] : (string * int) list list
```

To validate the function wordsort, we can proceed as follows:

```
wordsort [("type",2),("theory",1)];
> [("theory",1),("type",2)] : (string * int) list
```

and so on.

The operation of the function freq_count can also be validated:

```
freq_count (wordsort(concat(count_each(input ((open_in "data"), 1000))
                                                                   )))
>[("One",1),("There",1),("and",1),("calculate",1),("central",1),
      ("complexity",1),("enables",1),("find",1),("identify",1),("is",2),
                    ("it",1),("limits",1),...] : (string * int) list
```

If we want to validate freq_count using input from a file, and send the results to a file, then we must provide some auxiliary formatting functions. We will need to output the (word, frequency) pairs in a way which can be understood, so we will format each one with round brackets and commas, using a function called showpairs:

```
(*Pre: takes a list of pairs *)
(*Post: returns a list of strings *)
fun showpairs ((w,(n:int))::wcs) = "("^w^","^(makestring n)^") "::
                                                    (showpairs wcs)
  | showpairs [] = []
```

(Note that ^ is the standard string concatenation operator.)

We can now validate freq_count by taking the input from the file called data which was used earlier and sending the output to a file, f, as shown below:

```
format "f" (showpairs(freq_count (wordsort(concat(count_each(input
                                ((open_in "data"), 1000))))))))
```

The contents of f are now:

```
(One,1) (There,1) (and,1) (calculate,1) (central,1) (complexity,1)
(enables,1) (find,1) (identify,1) (is,3) (it,1) (limits,1) (main,1)
(measuring,1) (nature,1)(no,1) (of,4) (on,1) (or,1) (performance,1)
(problems,1) (process,1) (production,1) (progress,1) (size,1)
(software,2) (some,1) (that,1) (the,4) (theory,1) (to,4) (us,1)
(way,1) (which,1)
```

Finally, we can validate sort_and_count in a similar manner:

```
format "f" (showpairs(sort_and_count (input ((open_in "data"), 1000))))
```

which should produce the same results as above.

EXERCISES 2.2

1. Implement the following list processing functions:

```
val last : int list -> int
(*Post: returns the last (i.e. rightmost) item of the list *)

val isin : int -> int list -> bool
(*Post: return true if the given item is in list, otherwise false *)

val duplicate : int list -> int list
(*Post: returns a list in which each item is duplicated. For example,
   duplicate [1,2,3] should return [1,1,2,2,3,3] *)

val allout : int -> int list -> int list
(*Post:  returns a list in which all occurrences of the given item
   have been removed. *)

val firstout : int -> int list -> int list
(*Post:returns a list in which the first occurrence of the given item
   has been removed. *)

val replace : int -> int -> int list -> int list
(*Post: return a list in which the first occurrence of the 2nd
   parameter has been replaced by the 1st *)

val replaceall : int -> int -> int list -> int list
(*Post: return a list in which all occurrences of the 2nd parameter
   have been replaced by the 1st *)

val inbefore : int -> int -> int list -> int list
(*Post: return a list in which the 1st parameter has been inserted
   before every occurrence of the 2nd *)

val inaround : int -> int -> int list -> int list
(*Post: return a list in which the 1st parameter has been inserted
   before and after every occurrence of the 2nd *)
```

2. Rewrite the following expression to normal form:

```
bucketsort  [25, 36, 14, 9, 56, 21, 55, 72, 84, 93, 6, 51, 62, 75,
                                                     37, 12, 95]
```

3. Implement the function `shellsort`, the specification of which was given earlier.
4. Write a function to search the text for a keyword or phrase, to find the sentence which the phrase occurs in. (This is a variation of a *keyword in context search*). For example:

```
kwic "the worm" (read "sayings")
```

should return:

```
["The early bird catches the worm"]
```

if this phrase occurs in the file "sayings". All sentences which contain the phrase being searched for should be returned. (You may make the same assumptions about the format of the input as we did in our word counting examples.) To what extent can you reuse functions which have been introduced in this chapter?

SUMMARY

- The ADT *list* is a linear sequence of an arbitrary number of items of the same type together with a number of access functions.
- The five access functions are: `empty`, `cons`, `isempty`, `head` and `tail`. Of these, `empty` and `cons` are *constructor* functions, `isempty` is a *predicate* function and `head` and `tail` are *selector* functions.
- The algebraic specification of the ADT list consists of the syntax of the access functions, and six axioms which define their semantics.
- Lists are provided as standard data structures in most functional languages.
- A function which takes a function as a parameter (and possibly also returns one as its result) is called a *higher order function*. Higher order functions provide a framework within which software can be developed quickly and easily.
- A number of comparison sorts, implemented using lists, have been presented. The lower bound for the complexity of any comparison sort of n items is $O(n\log_2 n)$.

CHAPTER 3

Stacks

INTRODUCTION

In this chapter we consider the ADT *stack*. We start by giving a definition of the ADT, and then go on to specify it algebraically. We demonstrate how the methodology of data abstraction can be utilised in SML by means of the *abstype* construct and how generic ADTs can be fully realised by using parameterised modules (*functors*). We also analyse the advantages and disadvantages of both the type dependent and the generic implementations.

We start by giving a definition of the ADT.

DEFINITION

The ADT *stack* is a linear sequence of an arbitrary number of items (all of the same type) together with a number of access functions.

Note that the definition of the ADT stack is actually the same as that of the list. In fact the types stack and list are isomorphic, the only difference between the two being the nomenclature of the associated access functions.

REPRESENTATION AND NOTATION

The access functions are such that all insertions and deletions take place at one end of the sequence, called the *top*. The item most recently inserted on a stack is always the first to be removed. Consequently the stack has come to be known as a LIFO (Last In First Out) structure.

We will use the same representation for stacks as we did for the ADT list. So, for example,

The empty stack: ( )
A stack of words: ("hello", "world", "nice", "day")

The element at the top of the stack is the one furthest to the left, so, in the second example, the word "hello" is at the top. If we *pop* an element off the second stack we

47

will have a stack containing the words ("world", "nice", "day"). If we then *push* a new item on to the stack, the word "bye", say, we would have the stack ("bye", "world", "nice", "day").

As the ADT stack is considered to have a top it is usual to represent it diagrammatically as shown in Figure 3.1. The items are numbered according to the order they were put on the stack:

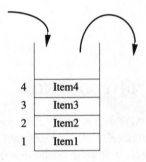

4	Item4
3	Item3
2	Item2
1	Item1

Figure 3.1

ALGEBRAIC SPECIFICATION

The algebraic specification of the ADT stack is equivalent to that of the list, the only difference being that the access function cons has been renamed push, head has become top and tail has been replaced by pop.

Syntax of the Access Functions

In the following specification we assume that the objects in the stack are of type item.

1. Constructor functions

We will need two constructor functions, empty and push, which have the following informal specifications, where Post is an abbreviation for *postcondition*:

```
val empty : stack
(*Post : returns an empty stack *)

val push : item -> stack -> stack
(*Post: returns a stack with the given item at the top *)
```

2. Predicate function

The only predicate function that we need is isempty:

```
val isempty : stack -> bool
(*Post: returns true if the stack is empty, otherwise false *)
```

3. Selector functions

The selector functions `top` and `pop` correspond to `head` and `tail` respectively:

```
val top : stack -> item
(*Post: returns the item at the top of the stack *)

val pop : stack -> stack
(*Post:  returns the stack obtained by removing the item at the top *)
```

Semantics of the Access Functions

The access functions must satisfy the following axioms, where x is an object of type `item` and xs is a stack:

```
1.  isempty empty = true
2.  isempty (push x xs) = false
3.  top empty   = error
4.  top (push x xs) = x
5.  pop empty = error
6.  pop (push x xs) = xs
```

As this specification is equivalent to that given for lists, the proofs of consistency and sufficient completeness are also very similar, and so will not be given again.

APPLICATIONS

The applications of stacks in computing are many and varied. Two examples are the allocation of run time memory in block structured languages which support the use of recursion (such as Pascal), and the parsing of arithmetic expressions.

The access functions can be considered to be an extension to our programming language, enabling us to construct software systems quickly and easily (see Figure 3.2).

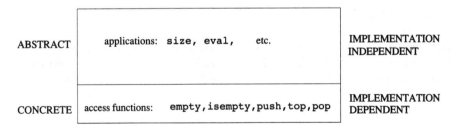

Figure 3.2

Examples

As a very simple example of the use of the access functions, consider the derivation of a function to determine the number of items on a stack. We can do this easily, using case analysis. If the stack is empty, then the answer is zero:

```
size xs = if isempty xs then 0
```

Otherwise, the answer is one more than the size of the stack without the item at the top, which we obtain by using the function pop:

```
else 1 + size (pop xs)
```

Putting these two cases together and adding the necessary syntactic constructs gives us the following SML function:

```
(*Post: returns the number of items on the stack *)
fun size xs = if isempty xs then 0
                 else 1 + size (pop xs)
```

As a second example, suppose that we want to write a simple postfix expression evaluator. Before doing this, we will explain the concepts of *infix*, *prefix* and *postfix* notation.

Infix notation is the conventional way of writing expressions, with the operators in between the operands. For example, denoting the operands by capital letters:

$$(A + B) * (C - D) \tag{1}$$

However, infix notation requires brackets to clarify expressions. If brackets were not used in the expression above, the multiplication might be assumed to apply to the operands B and C. Also, the order in which the operands and operators are written is not the order in which the computer requires them, that is, in which the operations are performed. With *postfix* notation each operator is placed immediately after the operands to which it applies. For example, expression (1) can be written using postfix notation as:

```
A B + C D - *
```

Postfix is also known as *Reverse Polish*.

Similarly, *prefix* notation means writing the operator before the appropriate operands. Using prefix notation, expression (1) becomes:

```
* + A B - C D
```

To transform a postfix expression to infix notation, we start reading from left to right, and stop when an operator is found. The operator must be placed between the last two operands which were read. Using brackets to clarify the translation from postfix to infix, this would give:

```
(A + B)  C D - *
```

followed by

```
(A + B)  (C - D) *
```

giving finally:

```
(A + B) * (C - D)
```

(To transform a prefix expression into an infix one, we follow a similar process, but read from right to left.)

A postfix expression evaluator might be needed in order to evaluate infix expressions, as it is easier to write a postfix evaluator than it is an infix one. An infix to postfix translator would then also be needed.

Let us assume that the postfix expressions that we wish to evaluate are very simple, in that they are correct (so we will not have to handle error cases) and they are composed only of integers and a selection of the four binary operators +, -,* and div. We will also assume that the postfix expression is stored as a list of strings. We must consider each object in the list, either pushing it on a stack (if it is an operand) or, if it is an operator, applying it to the top two integers on the stack, and pushing the result back on. For example, the postfix expression:

```
5 3 9 + *
```

would be stored in the input list as:

```
["5","3","9","+","*"]
```

We start by pushing the integers on the stack, and then encounter the addition symbol. Popping the top two operands from the stack and applying the operator to them gives us the result 12, which is then pushed on the stack. The next item in the list is a multiplication symbol, so we then pop the top two items on the stack, apply the operator to them, and again push the answer on the stack. So, at the end of the computation, the final solution to the evaluation will be at the top of the stack.

We will call our evaluation function eval. The top level function, evalpost, simply returns the item at the top of the stack, after calling eval with the expression to be evaluated and an empty stack:

```
fun evalpost xs = top (eval xs empty)
```

We can specify the function eval using pseudocode:

```
fun eval
(*Pre: takes a list and a stack which is empty initially *)
(*Post: returns the result of evaluating the expression stored in the
  list *)

if the input list is empty then return the stack
else
if the item at the head of the list is an operator then
     apply it to the top 2 operands and push the result on the stack
else
     push the value of the item on the stack
```

From the pseudocode, we can see that we will need a function which recognises operators. For our restricted set of operators, this is very simple to write:

```
fun isoperator x =  x = "+" orelse
                    x = "-" orelse
                    x = "*" orelse
                    x = "div"
```

As the integers are stored in the list as strings (because lists are homogeneous structures) we will need a function which returns the value of a string as an integer. We can implement this by using the function ord:

```
fun value x = ord x - ord "0"
```

and finally we also need a function which applies the operators to their arguments:

```
fun do_op "+" (a:int) b = a + b
  | do_op "-" a b = a - b
  | do_op "*" a b = a * b
  | do_op "div" a b = a div b
```

Now we can implement the eval function, using the pseudocode given earlier:

```
fun eval [] s = s
  | eval (x::xs) s = if isoperator x then
                        eval xs (push (do_op x (top (pop s))(top s))(pop
                                                                (pop s)))
                     else eval xs (push (value x) s)
```

Note that we did not need to know anything about the implementation of the access functions in order to develop these applications.

EXERCISE 3.1

1. Reduce the following expression to normal form:

```
evalpost ["7","2","3","5","*","-","+"]
```

IMPLEMENTATION

The next section demonstrates a simple implementation of the ADT stack, assuming that the items on the stack are integers. It is followed by a generic implementation of the ADT.

A Simple Implementation

ADTs in SML can be implemented by using the *abstype* mechanism. When used on its own this mechanism does not necessitate the use of a signature. However, after compiling the implementation of the ADT, the SML system will return the signature of the access functions, which must be declared between the with and end of the abstype definition. For example, a typical signature resulting from the implementation of the ADT stack is given below:

```
type stack
val empty = - : stack
val isempty = fn : stack -> bool
```

```
val push = fn : int -> stack -> stack
val top = fn : stack -> int
val pop = fn : stack -> stack
val showstack = fn : stack -> string
```

In addition to the access functions given in the algebraic specification, we have also included a function, showstack, which can be used to display the ADT.

As a simple prototype implementation, we will show how to implement a stack of integers by using a list. (Making the ADT type dependent violates our desires for generality, but is necessary to keep the implementation simple at this point: a generic stack implementation will be given later in the chapter.) The implementation of the type stack, using abstype, is given by:

```
abstype stack = Stack of int list
```

This indicates that the type constructor stack is implemented as a parameterised data type, using the data constructor Stack, which consists of a list of integers. That is, stack constructs a type, whereas Stack is a data object of type stack. We will use the convention of denoting the names of data constructors with an initial capital letter.

We can implement the constructor function empty by using a value declaration:

```
val empty = Stack []
```

The function isempty takes a parameter of type stack. Consequently, we must use the data constructor Stack in front of the variable which denotes the parameter. On the right hand side of this function definition we can use the implementation type, list, and compare the variable s (which is of type list) with an empty list:

```
fun isempty (Stack s) = s = []
```

For the constructor function, push, we simply use :: to add the element to the front of the list, and use the data constructor Stack to ensure that the result is of the right type:

```
fun push x (Stack xs) = Stack (x::xs)
```

The selector function top can be implemented by returning the head of the list:

```
fun top (Stack (x::xs)) = x
```

However, although this satisfies axiom 4 of the specification, we ought also to deal with axiom 3, which stated that taking the top of an empty stack should return an error. There are several ways that we could do this; one way is to try and take the head of an empty list:

```
fun top (Stack []) = hd []
```

which will generate the message:

```
uncaught exception Hd
```

whenever the error occurs. Thus, our function top is given by:

```
fun top (Stack []) = hd []
  | top (Stack (x::xs)) = x
```

Similarly, for the function pop, we either return the tail of the list (using the data constructor to turn it into a stack), or we cause an error to occur by taking the tail of an empty list:

```
fun pop (Stack []) = Stack (tl [])
  | pop (Stack (x::xs)) = Stack xs
```

Finally, we turn to the showstack function, which will be used to inspect instances of the ADT. We will do this by representing stacks by strings, with commas separating the elements in the stack:

```
fun showstack (Stack []) = ""
  | showstack (Stack (x::xs)) = makestring x ^
                         if not (xs = []) then
                             "," ^ showstack (Stack xs)
                         else  ""
```

The access functions must be placed between the keywords with and end; these words delimit the code within which stacks can be treated as lists. The complete implementation is given below:

```
abstype stack = Stack of int list

with

val empty = Stack []

fun isempty (Stack s) = s = []

fun push i (Stack s) = Stack (i::s)

fun top (Stack []) = hd []
  | top (Stack (s::ss)) = s

fun pop (Stack []) = Stack (tl [])
  | pop (Stack (s::ss)) = Stack ss

fun showstack (Stack []) = ""
  | showstack (Stack (s::ss)) = makestring s ^
                         if not (ss = []) then
                             "," ^ showstack (Stack ss)
                         else
                         ""

end
```

Verification and validation

The term *verification* will be used to mean the formal mathematical proof of a function's correctness, whereas *validation* refers to checking the correctness of a function by means of dynamic testing.

We can use the algebraic specification to guide the implementation of the ADT, and verify by observation that each access function satisfies the relevant part of the specification. Once the access functions have been implemented they can be validated, again using the axioms of the algebraic specification as an oracle (an authorative ruling). We can choose any arbitrary instance of a stack and use it in dynamic testing to check that the implementation corresponds to the specification. (This approach will be demonstrated for the following generic implementation.) The use of such verification and validation techniques is essential, as the access functions will be used and reused to construct hierarchies of software components.

Summary

One of the advantages of using abstype is that the implementation of the access functions is protected; the ADT can be treated as equivalent to its implementation type only between the with and end of the abstype definition. So the independence of the implementation is assured, guaranteeing one of the advantages of ADTs mentioned in Chapter 1.

Another advantage is that ADTs implemented using abstype are not equality types, which means that their instances cannot be tested for equality using the predefined equality function, and any attempt to do so will result in an error. This is important because intrinsic equality is structural equality, and so is inappropriate for use with ADTs, whose implementations are of secondary importance.

The lack of an implementor-defined signature for the ADT is the main disadvantage of using abstype as demonstrated in this section. A user of the ADT is forced to consult its implementation to ascertain its semantics, either by reading comments or by considering the code. However, it is possible to achieve a form of generic data abstraction in SML which overcomes this disadvantage, and may be more readily recognised by traditionalists, as we describe in the next section.

Generic Implementation

In imperative languages, such as Modula-2 and Ada, programmers using data abstraction can isolate all type-dependent functions, separating them from other functions in order to minimise the number of changes which must be made whenever types are changed. SML facilitates such modularisation and goes further, in that *functors* (parametrised modules) allow the instantiation of any number of different types within the same environment. This ability to define generic ADTs, combined with the use of the abstype mechanism (which ensures the protection of an ADT's implementation), gives us an impressive mechanism for producing reusable software.

For example, returning to the ADT stack, the functions which we must isolate are those access functions for the items in the stack which are type dependent. This includes a function, isequal, to compare two items for equality, so the type representing items must be an equality type. If we want to be able to display the contents of the items then we

must provide a function to do this (a function showitem, say). In order to output a stack
to a file we will also supply a formatting function which can be used to send the representation of a stack to a file. These considerations lead us to the following signature for the
items on the stack:

```
signature ITEM =
  sig
  eqtype item
  val isequal : item -> item -> bool
  (*Post: returns true if the items are equal *)
  val showitem : item -> string
  (*Post: a display function which returns a string *)
  val format : string -> string list -> unit
  (*Post: opens a file and outputs a list of strings to it *)
  end
```

Note that each function's signature is introduced by using the reserved word val,
rather than fun.

We will also define a signature for the ADT stack, containing the types of the access
functions which can be used to manipulate stacks. This signature will be used as a constraint on the implementation. The contents of a structure (which is simply a collection of
functions) can be accessed using dot notation, so I.item (for example) refers to the type
item of structure I.

```
signature STACK =
  sig
  structure I : ITEM
  type stack
  val empty : stack
  (*Post: returns an empty stack *)
  val isempty : stack -> bool
  (*Post: returns true if the stack is empty, otherwise false *)
  val push : I.item -> stack -> stack
  (*Post: returns a stack with the given item at the top *)
  val top : stack -> I.item
  (*Post: returns the item at the top of the stack *)
  val pop : stack -> stack
  (*Post: returns the stack obtained by removing the item at the top *)
  val showstack : stack -> string list
  (*Post: formats a stack for output *)
  end
```

Thus, the STACK signature is an accurate reflection of the syntactic part of the algebraic
specification of the ADT stack, and does not give any details about the implementation of
the ADT.

Now we define a functor (a parametrised collection of functions) which takes a structure with signature ITEM as a parameter. The functor heading is shown below, together
with the abstype declaration. The : STACK in the heading indicates that the functor is
constrained by the signature STACK.

```
functor MkStack (Itemstruct : ITEM) : STACK =
struct
```

```
structure I = Itemstruct   (*indiates that this item structure is the
                             same as that used in the signature*)

abstype stack = Stack of I.item list

with

etc.
```

The main body of the functor is identical to the simple stack implementation given earlier, except for the function showstack. This previously relied on the fact that the items on the stack were known to be integers, and so it had to be rewritten for the generic implementation. To prevent the function being type dependent, we will use the showitem function provided in the structure ITEM. As we do not know the size of the items in advance, it may be a good idea to represent the ADT as a list of strings (one per item); this will give us some flexibility when formatting the output.

Thus, the showstack function now becomes:

```
fun showstack (Stack []) = []
  | showstack (Stack (s::ss)) = (I.showitem s):: showstack (Stack ss)
```

Validating the generic ADT

To instantiate the functor MkStack so that we can test it we must provide structures of type ITEM, such as the one shown below, in which the items are instantiated as integers. The function showitem formats items as strings. The function format uses an auxiliary function showstring (provided in our library structure) to separate the strings in a list by chosen characters: here, we choose to start the output with the word stack followed by an opening brace, separate the strings by spaces, and place a closing brace at the end of the stack.

```
structure IntItem : ITEM =
  struct
  type item = int
  fun isequal a b = a = b
  fun showitem (a:item) = makestring a
  fun format f xs = output (open_out f, showstring "stack{" " " "}\n"
                                                                    xs)
  (*Post: opens a file f and outputs the list of strings xs to f,
     using showstring to format the output *)
  end
```

The function showstring helps us to format ADTs for output in a variety of ways, and is the main reason why the display function given within the implementing functor returns a list of strings, rather than a single string. This enables us to treat each item separately, adding commas (say) or new lines in between each one. The function is given below:

```
(*Pre: takes 3 strings and a list of strings *)
(*Post: returns a string, the result of adding fst to the front of the
   given list of string, mid between each list, last at the end and
   joining the lists together *)
```

```
fun showstring fst mid last xs = let fun show [ ] = [last]
                                      | show [y] = y::[last]
                                      | show (y::ys) = y::mid::(show
                                                                  ys)
                                  in fst ^ implode (show xs)
                                  end
```

Note the use of the function implode here, which (as explained in Chapter 2) takes a list of strings and concatenates them together into a single string.

We can form a structure IntStack by passing IntItem as a parameter to the functor MkStack:

```
structure IntStack = MkStack (IntItem)
```

If, however, the items on the stack are of type string, we will need to provide an alternative structure, such as the one shown below:

```
structure StringItem : ITEM =
  struct
  type item = string
  fun isequal a b = a = b
  fun showitem (a:item) = a
  fun format f xs = output (open_out f, showstring "stack{"
                                          "\n " "}\n" xs)
  (*Post: opens a file f and outputs the list of strings xs to f,
    using showstring to format the output *)
  end
```

and now we can form a structure StringStack using the structure StringItem:

```
structure StringStack = MkStack (StringItem)
```

The only differences between the StringItem structure and that given for IntItem are in the function format, which ensures (for the former) that each item (which is a string of unknown length) starts on a newline. However, we may choose to make the item type arbitrarily complicated, necessitating further changes. One of the advantages of using data abstraction is that these changes are isolated.

We can now test the access functions to check whether or not the implementation satisfies the algebraic specification. For example, consider axiom 4:

```
top (push x xs) = x
```

To ascertain whether or not this holds for stacks of strings, we could evaluate (using the StringStack structure) the following expression, which uses an arbitrary stack of names:

```
top (push "lml" (push "krc" (push "sml" (push "hope" empty))))
```

and check that it yields the answer "lml".

(Note: it is necessary to *open* the StringStack structure before evaluating the expression. Alternatively, we could prefix the access functions with the name of the structure followed by a dot.)

Similarly, to ascertain whether or not axiom 6:

```
pop (push x xs) = xs
```

holds, we could evaluate an expression of the form:

```
format "f" (showstack (pop (push "lml" (push "krc" (push "sml" (push
                                        "hope" empty))))))
```

which should result in the file f containing the following lines:

```
stack {krc
       sml
       hope}
```

Each of the axioms should be validated systematically, for each instantiation of the stack functor.

Applying the generic ADT

Functions which utilise the access functions (such as the size function, for example) can be defined within a functor which takes a structure of type STACK as a parameter. For example:

```
functor MkApplications (structure S : STACK) =
struct

open S          (* alternatively, dot notation can be used *)

(*Post: returns the number of items on the stack *)
fun size xs = if isempty xs then 0
                 else 1 + size (pop xs)

end
```

We can now instantiate the functor MkApplications by using one of the stack structures which we defined earlier. For example, for applications using stacks of integers, we could use a structure instantiated as shown below:

```
structure StringApplications = MkApplications (structure S = IntStack)
```

and, for applications using stacks of strings, we would form another structure:

```
structure StringApplications = MkApplications (structure S =
                                                StringStack)
```

If we open the structure StringApplications, we can then evaluate an expression of the form:

```
size (push "lml" (push "krc" (push "sml" (push "hope" empty))))
```

Structures can be instantiated with different types within the same environment by using the dot notation. For example, if we wanted to compare the number of items in a stack of integers with that in a stack of strings, then we could use an expression of the form:

```
IntApplications.size s1 = StringApplications.size s2
```

where s1 and s2 represent a stack of integers and a stack of strings, respectively.

Summary

The generic implementation has two advantages over the previous type dependent one:

- The functor is constrained by a signature which is defined by the implementor, and which acts as an interface to the ADT without giving any implementation details: consequently the ADT can be used without concern for its implementation, ensuring implementation independence.
- The functor is parametrised, facilitating the production of any number of different types of stacks, ensuring that the software has a high potential for reuse.

SUMMARY

- The ADT *stack* is a linear sequence of an arbitrary number of items (all of the same type) together with the access functions empty, push, isempty, top and pop.
- The types stack and list are isomorphic.
- The applications of stacks in computing are many and varied; two examples are the allocation of run time memory in block structured languages which support the use of recursion, and the parsing of arithmetic expressions.
- The use of abstype enables us to protect the implementation of the access functions, assuring the independence of the implementation. Also, abstype protects instances of the ADT from being tested for structural equality. On its own, however, the use of abstype does not provide an interface for the ADT. By encapsulating the ADT within a functor constrained by a signature we can overcome this disadvantage.
- Programming using functors (parametrised modules) enables us to write reusable, generic software.

CHAPTER 4

Queues

INTRODUCTION

In this chapter we discuss the ADT queue. After giving its definition and algebraic specification, we go on to consider possible generic implementations. We finish the chapter by looking at two different variations of the ADT queue, *priority queues* and *dequeues*.

DEFINITION

The ADT *queue* is a linear sequence of an arbitrary number of items (of the same type) together with a number of access functions.

Note that the definition of the ADT queue, like that of the stack, is actually the same as that of the ADT list. However, the access functions are such that additions are only allowed at the *back* of the queue, in contrast with lists and stacks which only allowed additions at the front. Consequently queues are known as FIFO (First-In-First-Out) structures.

REPRESENTATION AND NOTATION

We will adopt the same representation for queues as we did for stacks. So, for example,

The empty queue: ( )
A queue of names: ("Jane", "Pam", "Sue")

We use the convention that the item at the front of the queue is the leftmost one, so (for example) the item at the front of the second queue is "Jane", and the item at the back of the queue is "Sue". If we add a new item to the second queue, the name "Carol", say, the result would be the queue ("Jane", "Pam", "Sue", "Carol").

ALGEBRAIC SPECIFICATION

We will start by giving the algebraic specification for the ADT. This consists of the syntax and semantics of the access functions. The specification assumes that the objects in the queue are of type item.

Syntax of the Access Functions

1. Constructor functions

As usual, we need two constructor functions, which we will call empty and add:

```
val empty : queue
(*Post: returns an empty queue *)

val add : item -> queue -> queue
(*Post: returns a queue with the given item added at the back *)
```

2. Predicate function

We need a predicate function, isempty, which will test whether or not a queue is empty:

```
val isempty : queue -> bool
(*Post: returns true if the queue is empty, false otherwise *)
```

3. Selector functions

The selector functions front and back return the item at the front of a queue and the queue without the front item, respectively:

```
val front : queue -> item
(*Post: returns the  item at the front of the queue  *)

val back : queue -> queue
(*Post: returns a queue without the  item at the front  *)
```

Semantics of the Access Functions

The access functions must satisfy the following set of axioms, where x is an object of type item and xs is a queue. The first three axioms are self-explanatory.

```
1.  isempty empty = true
2.  isempty (add x xs) = false
3.  front empty  = error
```

The fourth axiom specifies the behaviour of the access function front with a non-empty queue:

```
4.  front (add x xs) = if isempty xs then x else front xs
```

Axiom 4 states that if we add an item x to the back of an empty queue, then it must also be at the front of the queue, and so we should return that item. Otherwise, we ignore the item x (since it is at the back of the queue) and query to find the item at the front of xs. Since xs is not empty, it is of the form (add x' xs'), where xs' is a queue and x' is an item. If xs' is empty, then x' is the item at the front of xs and we have finished. Otherwise we must ask what item is at the front of xs', and so on.

The final two axioms specify the behaviour of the access function back:

5. back empty = error
6. back (add x xs) = if isempty xs then empty else add x (back xs)

Axiom 6 says that if we add an item x to a queue which is empty, then x becomes the front of the queue, and so the back of the queue (which is the result of removing the item at the front of the queue) is the empty queue. Otherwise we must add x to the result of finding the back of xs. Now, as before, x is of the form add xs′ x′. If xs′ is empty, then we return the empty queue (because x′ is the item at the front of xs), and so the result is the queue with x in it. Otherwise we must add x′ to the result of finding the back of xs′, and so on.

For example, the evaluation of a call to determine the back of a queue with three numbers in it proceeds as follows, where the queue is denoted by round brackets:

```
back (1, 2, 3) → back (add 3 (1, 2))
               → add 3 (back (1, 2))
               → add 3 (add 2 (back (1)))
               → add 3 (add 2 (back (add 1 empty)))
               → add 3 (add 2 empty)
               → add 3 (2)
               → (2, 3)
```

We also require the access functions to be strict, that is, to return an error value if an error is passed to them as a parameter.

As this specification is similar to that given for lists, so too are the proofs of consistency and sufficient completeness, which are omitted.

APPLICATIONS

Applications for queues include allocation of resources by operating systems on multi-user machines (such as printers, disk access, processor time), and simulation of real world queuing. There are several well-known scheduling algorithms which are implemented using the ADT queue. For example, the round-robin algorithm for items which are competing for a resource uses a circular queue, in which an item is taken from the front of a queue, given a certain amount of time and is then returned to the back of the queue. Short jobs will finish quickly and be removed from the queue, whereas longer jobs will need several cycles to complete.

The examples below show how the access functions can be treated as basic constructs in our extended language (see Figure 4.1).

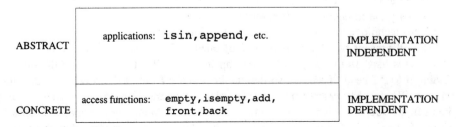

Figure 4.1

Examples

As a simple example of the use of the access functions to develop functions which manipulate queues, consider the derivation of a function to check a queue for the presence of a particular item. (This function could be of use if we wanted to make sure that no item is inserted into a queue twice.)

We can derive the function by case analysis. If the queue is empty then we return `false`, otherwise we check the item at the front of the queue to see if it is the one that we want. If it is, we return `true`, otherwise we call the function again to check the rest of the queue. The function is given below:

```
(*Post: returns true if the given item is contained in the given queue*)
fun isin qs i = if isempty qs then false
                else
                if (I.isequal) (front qs) i then true
                else
                isin (back qs) i
```

Here, `isequal` is a boolean valued function which takes two items and returns *true* if they are equal and *false* otherwise. This function is used for generality, as we do not want to force the applications to depend on a particular type of item. We have assumed that `isequal` has been implemented within a structure which matches the ITEM signature, and which is referred to by `I` (and so can be accessed using `I.isequal`).

Now consider a function to append two queues. This could be of use, for example, if there are two queues for one resource, and one queue has higher priority than the other. The items at the front of the second queue will be added to the back of the first:

```
(*Post: returns the result of joining the second queue to the back of
   the first *)
fun append q1 q2 = if isempty q2 then q1
                   else
                   append (add (front q2) q1) (back q2)
```

As usual, we have constructed these higher level functions by using the access functions, without any concern for the implementation of the ADT.

IMPLEMENTATION

In the previous chapter we discussed a method of developing generic ADTs which involved the use of functors. In view of the advantages that such an approach gives us (particularly the modularity and reusability of the resulting code), we will concentrate on using this technique throughout the remainder of the book.

We will present two implementations of queues. The first is a naive implementation which uses lists. In this implementation, an item is added to the back of the queue by adding it to the head of the list, so that the item at the front of the queue is at the end of the list. We start by isolating the type dependent functions, to produce a signature for the items in the queue. (This part of the process is common to both of our queue implementations.) In fact, we can reuse the signature for items which we presented in the previous chapter:

```
signature ITEM =
  sig
  eqtype item
  val isequal : item -> item -> bool
  (*Post: returns true if the items are equal *)
  val showitem : item -> string
  (*Post: a display function which returns a string *)
  val format : string -> string list -> unit
  (*Post: opens a file and outputs a list of strings to it *)
end
```

We also need to define a signature for the ADT queue, containing the types of the access functions. This will be used to constrain the functor, ensuring that the implementation matches the signature:

```
signature QUEUE =
  sig
  structure I : ITEM
  type queue
  val empty : queue
  (*Post: returns an empty queue *)
  val isempty : queue -> bool
  (*Post: returns true if the queue is empty, false otherwise *)
  val add : I.item -> queue -> queue
  (*Post: returns a queue with the given item added at the back *)
  val front : queue -> I.item
  (*Post: returns the  item at the front of the queue  *)
  val back : queue -> queue
  (*Post: returns a queue without the  item at the front  *)
  val showqueue : queue -> string list
  (*Post: formats a queue for output *)
end
```

(Note that as well as the access functions, we also intend to provide a showqueue function, so that we can inspect instances of the ADT.)

A Sample Implementation using Lists

Now we can implement the access functions, using a functor called MkQueue. The functor heading and abstype declaration have the following form:

```
functor MkQueue (Itemstruct : ITEM) : QUEUE =
struct
structure I = Itemstruct    (*indicates that this item structure is the
                             same as that used in the signature*)

abstype queue = Queue of  I.item list
```

We have declared a type constructor, queue, by using a data constructor, Queue. The functor is constrained by the signature QUEUE, and uses a parameter Itemstruct, which is a structure with signature ITEM.

We will implement the constructor function empty by using a value declaration. Note that the data constructor Queue is needed on the right hand side of the equation to ensure that the empty list is treated as a queue.

```
val empty = Queue []
```

The function `isempty` can be implemented by comparing its parameter xs (which is a list when not coupled with the data constructor Queue) with an empty list:

```
fun isempty (Queue xs) = xs = []
```

To implement the constructor function `add`,we simply cons the item onto the front of the list, and use the data constructor Queue to reform the queue:

```
fun add x (Queue xs) = Queue (x::xs)
```

As we have implemented `add` is this way, our implementation of the function `front` can reflect its algebraic specification (axioms 3 and 4). We ensure that an error occurs if the function is called with an empty queue by calling the function hd with an empty list. If the queue only contains one item, then this is the item at the front. Otherwise, we ignore the most recently added item and search for the item at the front of the rest of the queue. The implementation of `front` is given below; again, the data constructor Queue is needed whenever the list is to be treated as a queue.

```
fun front (Queue []) = hd []
  | front (Queue (x::xs)) = if isempty (Queue xs) then x
                            else front (Queue xs)
```

The function `back` can also be implemented by using the algebraic specification (axioms 5 and 6) as a guide. This implementation directly reflects the specification.

```
fun back (Queue []) = Queue (tl [])
  | back (Queue (x::xs)) = if isempty (Queue xs) then empty
                           else add x (back (Queue xs))
```

We will implement the `showqueue` function in a similar manner to `showstack`, with queues being represented as lists of strings. As the queue is stored in the list in reverse, we must reverse the items as they are processed, so that the item at the front of the queue is the leftmost string in the list which is output. Thus the item at the head of the list must be appended to the result of displaying the rest of the queue. We use the function `showitem`, which is taken from the structure with signature ITEM that was passed as a parameter to the functor.

```
fun showqueue (Queue []) = []
  | showqueue (Queue (x::xs)) = showqueue (Queue xs) @ [I.showitem x]
```

The entire implementation is given below:

```
functor MkQueue (Itemstruct : ITEM) : QUEUE =
struct
structure I = Itemstruct    (*indicates that this item structure is the
                              same as that used in the signature*)

abstype queue = Queue of  I.item list
```

```
with

val empty = Queue []

fun isempty (Queue xs) = xs = []

fun add x (Queue xs) = Queue (x::xs)

fun front (Queue []) = hd []
  | front (Queue (x::xs)) = if isempty (Queue xs) then x
                                 else front (Queue xs)

fun back (Queue []) = Queue (tl [])
  | back (Queue (x::xs)) = if isempty (Queue xs) then empty
                                else add x (back (Queue xs))

fun showqueue (Queue []) = []
  | showqueue (Queue (x::xs)) = showqueue (Queue xs) @ [I.showitem x]

end

end
```

Summary

The advantage of this implementation is that adding an item to the queue is very efficient; it can be done in constant time, i.e. $O(1)$. However, finding the item at the front of the queue is not so efficient, being an $O(n)$ operation, for a queue of n items.

An Implementation using a Pair of Lists

Our second implementation for the ADT uses a pair of lists (Burton 1982).

The first list in the pair holds the items which are closest to the front of the queue in such a way that the item at the front of the queue is at the head of the list. The second list in the pair stores the items which are closest to the back of the queue, in the opposite order to the first list; that is, items can be added to the back of the queue by inserting them into the front of this list using :: (cons). If the first list in the pair becomes empty, it is replaced by the reverse of the second list.

The functor heading and abstype declaration are given below:

```
functor MkQueue  (Itemstruct : ITEM) : QUEUE =
struct
structure I = Itemstruct

abstype queue = Queue of  ((I.item) list) * ((I.item)list)
```

The constructor function empty returns a queue constructed from two empty lists:

```
val empty = Queue ([],[])
```

The predicate function isempty must check that both lists are empty:

```
fun isempty (Queue (xs,ys)) = (xs = []) andalso (ys = [])
```

In order to ensure that the first list (which gives us access to the front of the queue) always contains an item if the queue is not empty, we need an auxiliary function which ensures that if this list becomes empty, it is replaced by the second list. We will call this function normalise. Note that it is private to the implementation of the ADT, because it is not declared in the QUEUE signature.

```
fun normalise (Queue (xs,ys)) = if xs = [] then
                                    Queue (reverse ys, [])
                                 else
                                    Queue (xs,ys)
```

This function uses a function called reverse, which is part of our library of generally applicable functions. Its implementation is shown below:

```
fun reverse [] = []
  | reverse (x::xs) = reverse xs @ [x]
```

Using the normalise function, we can implement what remains of the access functions. For the function add, we insert the new item into the second list, using ::, and then call normalise:

```
fun add x (Queue (xs,ys)) = normalise (Queue (xs, (x::ys)))
```

The selector function front can be implemented by case analysis on the possible forms which a queue can have, using axioms 3 and 4 of the algebraic specification:

```
fun front (Queue ([],[])) = hd []
  | front (Queue (x::xs,ys)) = x
  | front (Queue ([],ys)) = front (normalise (Queue ([],ys)))
```

Similarly, we can implement the function back, by considering axioms 5 and 6 and the possible structure of the queue:

```
fun back (Queue ([],[])) = Queue (tl [], [])
  | back (Queue ([],ys)) = back  (normalise (Queue ([],ys)))
  | back (Queue (x::xs,ys)) = Queue (xs,ys)
```

Finally, the display function, showqueue, which formats a queue as a list of strings (one string per item), can also be defined by using case analysis on the different forms the queue can take:

```
fun showqueue (Queue ([],[])) = []
  | showqueue (Queue ([],ys))  = showqueue (normalise (Queue ([],ys)))
  | showqueue (Queue (x::xs,ys)) = [I.showitem x] @ showqueue (Queue
                                                                   (xs,ys))
```

Summary

The advantage of using this technique is that it gives us (on average) constant time access to both the front and the back of the queue. However, the disadvantage is that the relationship between the algebraic specification and the implementation of the access functions is no longer immediately obvious.

Verification and Validation

We can verify the two generic implementations against the algebraic specification by rewriting calls to the predicate and selector functions with both an empty queue and an arbitrary instance of a queue. The first implementation has an advantage here over the second because it directly reflects the algebraic specification of the access functions, leading to a very a straightforward verification.

In order to validate the implementations, we have to provide a structure of type ITEM, such as the following integer structure:

```
structure IntItem : ITEM =
  struct
  type item = int
  fun isequal a b = a = b
  fun showitem (a:item) = makestring a
  fun format f xs = output (open_out f, showstring "queue{" " " "}\n"
                                                               xs)
  (*Post: opens a file f and outputs the list of strings xs to f,
    using showstring to format the output *)
  end
```

Now we can pass this structure as a parameter to the MkQueue functor, to produce an implementation for queues of integers:

```
structure IntQueue = MkQueue (IntItem)
```

Similarly, we could instantiate the items as strings:

```
structure StringItem : ITEM =
  struct
  type item = string
  fun isequal a b = a = b
  fun showitem (a:item) = a
  fun format f xs = output (open_out f, showstring "queue{" "\n    " "}
                                                               \n" xs)
  (*Post: opens a file f and outputs the list of strings xs to f,
    using showstring to format the output *)
  end
```

and then provide a structure for queues of strings:

```
structure StringQueue = MkQueue (StringItem)
```

We can now validate the access functions, using the algebraic specification as an oracle to predict the outcome of the tests.

For example, to validate axiom 6, we could evaluate an expression of the form:

```
showqueue (back (add 3 (add 4 (add 5 (add 6 empty)))))
```

and check the result against that predicted by the algebraic specification:

```
["5","4","3"] : string list
```

In order to ascertain the correctness of the ADT's implementation, each of the access functions should be validated in this manner, using the algebraic specification to predict the results. Having performed this task for one instantiation of the ADT, it is simple to re-run the tests each time a queue with a different type of item is constructed.

Applying the Generic ADT

In order to keep the software well modularised, we will encapsulate the applications which use the access functions within a functor. To implement the applications which we discussed earlier, we will need a functor which takes two parameters, one of type ITEM and the other of type QUEUE (because functions from structures of both these types are required), such as the functor shown below:

```
functor MkApplications (structure I : ITEM and Q: QUEUE) =
   struct

   open Q                       (* an alternative to using dot notation *)

   (*Post: returns true if the given item is contained in the given
      queue *)
   fun isin qs i = if isempty qs then false
                   else
                   if (I.isequal) (front qs) i then true
                   else
                   isin (back qs) i

   (*Post: returns the result of joining the second queue to the back
      of the first *)
   fun append q1 q2 = if isempty q2 then q1
                      else
                      append (add (front q2) q1) (back q2)

   end
```

We can instantiate this functor by using an item and a queue structure. For example, if we want to apply the above functions to queues of integers, then we could form a structure called IntApps by using the following statement:

```
structure IntApps = MkApplications (structure I = IntItem and Q =
                                                              IntQueue)
```

EXERCISE 4.1

1. Reduce the following expression to normal form, showing all working:

```
isin  (add 3 (add 4 (add 5 (add 6 empty)))) 6
```

PRIORITY QUEUES

Sometimes the ADT queue is not sufficiently structured. Some problems require different items to be given different priorities, depending on some notion of their merit. For these problems, a *priority queue* may be needed. The definition of this ADT is given below.

DEFINITION

The ADT *priority queue* is a linear sequence of an arbitrary number of ordered items, all of the same type, together with a number of access functions.

Such a queue is also called an *ordered* queue. A priority queue is similar in functionality to a queue except in the case of insertion: an item is inserted in the queue according to its priority, and not (in general) at the back of the queue. When an item is inserted it is placed after all items of the same priority, but before any item of lower priority. For example, if we have data items x, y, and z, with respective priorities of 29, 14 and 26 (where the highest priority is denoted by the largest number), then the priority queue could be represented by:

```
((x,29),(z,26),(y,14))
```

This ADT does not really qualify to be called a queue, since insertion is not necessarily at the back of the sequence. Its functionality resembles that of a list, rather than that of a queue.

ALGEBRAIC SPECIFICATION

The algebraic specification of the priority queue is very similar to that of the queue. The differences between the specifications arise due to the semantics of the function which constructs non-empty queues.

Syntax of the Access Functions

1. Constructor functions

In the following specification, we assume that the ADT is called priorityq. There are two constructor functions, empty and insert:

```
val empty : priorityq
(*Post: returns an empty queue *)

val insert :  item -> priorityq -> priorityq
(*Post: returns a priority queue with the given item inserted in the
  correct position *)
```

2. Predicate function

We also have two predicate functions:

```
val isempty : priorityq -> bool
(*Post: returns true if the priority queue is empty, otherwise false *)

val isgreater: item -> item -> bool
(*Post: returns true if the 1st item has greater priority than the 2nd*)
```

3. Selector functions

The selector functions are the same as those for queues:

```
val front : priorityq -> item
(*Post: returns the  item at the front of the priority queue*)

val back : priorityq -> priorityq
(*Post: returns a priority queue without the  item at the front  *)
```

Semantics of the Access Functions

1. isempty empty = true
2. isempty (insert x xs) = false
3. front empty = error
4. front (insert x xs) = if isgreater x (front xs) or isempty xs
   then x else front xs
5. back empty = error
6. back (insert x xs) = if isgreater x (front xs) or isempty xs
   then xs else (back xs)
7. isgreater x y = x > y

APPLICATIONS

There are many applications for priority queues in the area of resource allocation for multi-user operating systems. For example, the items may be processes (programs in execution) which must be scheduled for processor time.

A multi-level queue has a top priority queue which all jobs join initially. Jobs which are not completed within a certain amount of time are then relegated to a second queue which is served less frequently and are then only given limited amounts of time. Such queues are common in schedulers for timesharing systems.

The number of different values of priority in a priority queue depends on the problem being solved. For some applications (such as the queue for a central processing unit) it may be best to have a large number of different priorities, whereas for applications such as queues for printers it may be enough to have only a few priorities (for example, high, medium and low). In this case it may be best to have several subqueues, each of which holds items which have the same priority. Items are added to the end of the appropriate subqueue, and are removed from the front of the subqueue. For such structures, fast access may be needed for both the front and back of the subqueues. In more complicated schedulers, the priority may be a function of the time the item has spent in the queue as well as its importance.

IMPLEMENTATION

In order to implement priority queues, we will use a constraint signature for the priority queue functor of the following form:

```
signature PRIORITYQ =
  sig
  structure I : ITEM
  type priorityq
  val empty : priorityq
  (*Post: returns an empty priority queue *)
  val isempty : priorityq -> bool
  (*Post: returns true if the priority queue is empty, otherwise
    false *)
  val insert : I.item -> priorityq -> priorityq
  (*Post: returns a priority queue with the given item inserted in the
    correct position *)
  val front : priorityq -> I.item
  (*Post: returns the item at the front of the given priority queue *)
  val back : priorityq -> priorityq
  (*Post: returns a priority queue without the item at the front *)
  val showpriorityq : priorityq -> string list
  (*Post: formats a priority queue for output  *)
  end
```

Note that we no longer have the access function add, but instead we have a constructor function called insert. This will insert an item in the correct position in the priority queue, according to its merit. Also the function isgreater will be added to the item structures.

An implementation using lists is straightforward: if we ensure that the front of the priority queue is stored at the head of the list then this will give us constant time access to the item with largest priority. Similarly, we will also have constant time access to the back of the queue.

The only access function which requires some ingenuity is the insert function. To ensure that the item is placed in the correct position, we will use the comparison function isgreater, which must be implemented within the structures with signature ITEM. We will also use a local function called order, which (because it is defined within the implementing functor) will treat the queue as a list. As this function uses a linear search to find the correct position for the insertion, its time complexity is $O(n)$ for a queue of n items.

```
fun insert i (PriorityQ []) =  PriorityQ [i]
  | insert i (PriorityQ (q::qs)) = let fun order x (y::ys) =
                                  if I.isgreater x y then
                                  (x::(y::ys))
                                  else (y::order x ys)
                                    | order x [] = [x]
                                in PriorityQ (order i (q::qs))
                                end
```

The entire implementation is given below:

```
functor MkPriorityQ (Itemstruct : ITEM) : PRIORITYQ =
struct
structure I = Itemstruct

abstype priorityq = PriorityQ of  I.item list

with

val empty = PriorityQ []

fun isempty (PriorityQ qs) = qs = []

fun front (PriorityQ []) = hd []
  | front (PriorityQ (q::qs)) = q

fun back (PriorityQ []) = PriorityQ (tl [])
  | back (PriorityQ (q::qs)) = PriorityQ qs

(*Post: inserts an item into the correct position in the priority
   queue *)
fun insert i (PriorityQ []) =  PriorityQ [i]
  | insert i (PriorityQ (q::qs)) = let fun order x (y::ys) =
                                         if I.isgreater x y then
                                         (x::(y::ys))
                                         else (y::order x ys)
                                           | order x [] = [x]
                                     in PriorityQ (order i (q::qs))
                                     end

fun showpriorityq (PriorityQ []) = []
  | showpriorityq (PriorityQ (q::qs)) =I.showitem q::showpriorityq
                                               (PriorityQ qs)

end

end
```

A signature for items in the priority queue will need to include the comparison function
isgreater which is used by insert. A typical signature is given below.

```
signature ITEM =
  sig
  eqtype item
  val isequal : item -> item -> bool
  (*Post: returns true if the items have the same priorities *)
  val isless : item -> item -> bool
  (*Post: returns true if the 1st item has lower priority than the
     2nd *)
  val isgreater : item -> item -> bool
  (*Post: returns true if the 1st item has greater priority than the
     2nd
```

```
    val showitem : item -> string
    (*Post: a display function which returns a string *)
    val format : string -> string list -> unit
    (* Post: opens a file and outputs a list of strings to it *)
  end
```

To instantiate this signature, we will use a structure called StringIntItem, in which we have assumed that an item consists of a (string, integer) pair, where the integer represents the priority of the string. The comparison functions compare the priorities of two items.

```
structure StringIntItem : ITEM =
  struct
  type item = (string * int)
  fun isequal (s1,i:int) (s2,j) = i = j
  fun isless (s1,i:int) (s2,j) = i < j
  fun isgreater (s1,i:int) (s2,j) = i > j
  fun showitem (s,i:int) = "(" ^ s ^ "," ^ makestring i ^ ")"
  fun format f xs = output (open_out f, showstring "queue{" " " "}\n"
                                                                    xs)
  (*Post: opens a file f and outputs the list of strings xs to f,
    using showstring to format the output *)
  end
```

We can instantiate a priority queue structure, using the MkPriorityQ functor, as shown below:

```
structure StringPriorityQ = MkPriorityQ (StringIntItem)
```

If we now open the StringPriorityQ and StringIntItem structures, we can evaluate a statement of the form:

```
format "f1" (showpriorityq (insert ("jane",9) (insert ("pam",1)
                           (insert ("sue",5) (insert ("anne", 2)
                           empty)))))
```

to obtain the result:

```
queue{(jane,9) (sue,5) (anne,2) (pam,1)}
```

We will consider a more efficient implementation of priority queues in Chapter 6.

DEQUEUES

The last and most flexible ADT we discuss in this chapter is called a *double-ended* queue or *dequeue* for short. Such queues allow insertion and deletion at both ends of the sequence. The algebraic specification for the ADT dequeue is given below. It assumes the existence of a structure I with signature ITEM. There are now three constructor functions, empty, rightcons and leftcons, and consequently we must specify the semantics of the selector and predicate functions for each of these cases.

Syntax

```
signature DEQUEUE =
  sig
  structure I : ITEM
  type dequeue
  val empty : dequeue
  (*Post:  returns an empty queue *)
  val isempty : dequeue -> bool
  (*Post:  returns true if the dequeue is empty *)
  val leftcons : I.item -> dequeue -> dequeue
  (*Post:  returns a dequeue with item I added on the left of the
    dequeue *)
  val rightcons : I.item -> dequeue -> dequeue
  (*Post:  returns a dequeue with item I added on the right of the
    dequeue *)
  val left : dequeue -> I.item
  (*Post:  returns the leftmost item in the dequeue *)
  val right : dequeue -> I.item
  (*Post:  returns the rightmost item in the dequeue *)
  val lefttail : dequeue -> dequeue
  (*Post:  returns a dequeue without the leftmost item *)
  val righttail : dequeue -> dequeue
  (*Post: returns a dequeue without the rightmost item *)
  val showdequeue : dequeue -> string list
    (*Post: formats a priority queue for output  *)
  end
```

Semantics

1.   isempty empty = true
2.   isempty right cons i q = false
3.   isempty leftcons i q = false
4.   right empty = error
5.   right (rightcons i q) = i
6.   right (leftcons i q) = if isempty q then i else (right q)
7.   left empty = error
8.   left (leftcons i q) = i
9.   left (rightcons i q) = if isempty q then i else (left q)
10. righttail empty = error
11. righttail (rightcons i q) = q
12. righttail (leftcons i q) = if isempty q then empty
                                 else (leftcons i (righttail q))
13. lefttail empty = error
14. lefttail (leftcons i q) = q
15. lefttail (rightcons i q) = if isempty q then empty
                                 else (rightcons i (lefttail q))

As usual we assume that the access functions are strict, that is, they return an error if passed an error parameter.

Dequeues may be input-restricted, allowing input at one end only, or output-restricted, allowing output at one end only. Some applications that use this ADT may not need the full power of a dequeue but simply the ability to put some items at the front of the queue. Like the priority queue, this structure does not really qualify to be called a queue because it does not exhibit FIFO behaviour.

The implementation of the access functions is left as an exercise for the reader.

EXERCISE 4.2

1. Provide an implementation of the ADT dequeue.

SUMMARY

- The ADT *queue* is a linear sequence of an arbitrary number of items (of the same type) together with a number of access functions.
- The access functions (`empty`, `add`, `isempty`, `front` and `back`) are such that additions are only allowed at the back of a queue, and deletions from the front.
- The ADT *priority queue* is a linear sequence of an arbitrary number of ordered items, all of the same type, together with a number of access functions.
- Priority queues are also called *ordered* queues.
- The ADT *dequeue* is a double ended queue in which insertion and deletion are allowed at both ends of the sequence.

CHAPTER 5

Binary Trees

INTRODUCTION

The ADTs which we have discussed so far (lists, stacks and queues) all have a linear ordering imposed on their items, in that each item can have at most one predecessor and one successor. Consequently such ADTs are said to be *linear*. The ADT which we are going to discuss in this chapter, the *binary tree*, is *non-linear* in that each item is allowed to have as many as two successors. Such ADTs allow us to express more general relationships between the components of a compound structure.

We describe some of the properties of this ADT and introduce the terminology which has come to be associated with it. The different methods of traversing a tree are also discussed together with examples of their use. We show how to implement the higher order functions map and fold for this ADT, and finally we demonstrate how trees can be implemented.

The definition of a binary tree is given below.

DEFINITION

The ADT *binary tree* is a finite set of nodes which is either empty or consists of a data item (called the *root*) and two disjoint binary trees (called the *left* and the *right subtrees* of the root), together with a number of access functions.

We will occasionally refer to a *binary tree* simply as a *tree*, if the full meaning can be inferred from the context.

If we restrict the nodes in a binary tree to be arranged in the tree in some order, then the result is a *binary search tree*, or *ordered binary tree*, which is the subject of the next chapter. An ADT which is more general than the binary tree is an *n-ary* tree, in which an item may have more than two subtrees.

We start by introducing some notation.

REPRESENTATION AND NOTATION

There are several ways that we can represent a tree. The hierarchical representation that is used in Figure 5.1 shows the data item at the root of the tree (which is drawn at the top of the diagram) and the left and right subtrees (the resemblance to an inverted botanical tree is what gives the ADT its name). The root is sometimes referred to as the *parent* of its subtrees.

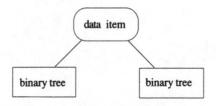

Figure 5.1

For example, a tree of characters is shown in Figure 5.2. The nodes which do not have any successors are called *leaves* or *terminal nodes*. In Figure 5.2 the leaves contain the characters K, F, and S.

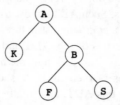

Figure 5.2

As an alternative to the graphical representation used in Figure 5.2, we could flatten the tree to produce a bracketed tuple with the left subtree as first component, followed by the root, followed by the right subtree. The representation of each of the subtrees follows the same format, so that the structure of the tree is not lost. For example, the tree in Figure 5.2 would be flattened to:

```
((K), A, ((F), B, (S)))
```

The algebraic specification for the ADT is given in the next section.

ALGEBRAIC SPECIFICATION

There are six access functions for the ADT binary tree. As usual, we will specify their syntax before giving their semantics.

Syntax of the Access Functions

The two constructor functions are called empty and cons. The latter takes an item and two trees and constructs a tree with the item at the root, and the two trees as its left and right subtrees.

```
val empty : tree
(*Post: returns an empty tree *)

val cons : item -> tree -> tree -> tree
(*Pre: takes an item i and two trees l and r
  Post: returns a new tree which has the given item at its root and
  the 2 trees as its left and right subtrees *)
```

The predicate function which is used to test a tree to see if it is empty is called isempty:

```
val isempty : tree -> bool
(*Post: returns true if the tree is empty, otherwise false *)
```

There are three selector functions called root, left and right which select the value at the root, the left subtree and right subtree respectively.

```
val root : tree -> item
(*Post : returns the data item at the root of the tree  *)

val left : tree -> tree
(*Post : returns the left subtree of tree *)

val right : tree -> tree
(*Post : returns the right subtree of tree *)
```

Semantics of the Access Functions

We can derive the axioms for the access functions by noticing that a binary tree is either empty or of the form (cons i l r), where i is an item and l and r are the left and right subtrees respectively. The semantics of the access functions are entirely analogous to those for the ADTs previously discussed; for example, just as trying to find the head of an empty list results in an error, so does trying to find the root of an empty tree (as indicated by axiom 3).

```
1.  isempty empty = true
2.  isempty (cons i l r) = false
3.  root empty  = error
4.  root (cons i l r) = i
5.  left empty  = error
6.  left (cons i l r) = l
7.  right empty  = error
8.  right (cons i l r) = r
```

APPLICATIONS

Non-linear data types are useful in simulating one to many relationships. They can be used to implement a number of other abstract data types, such as sets. Trees are often used during the syntax analysis stage of compilation to parse expressions, in which case they are referred to as *parse* trees. For example, the tree in Figure 5.3 represents the statement:

```
x = y + z * 5
```

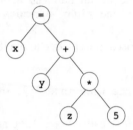

Figure 5.3

The example given next shows how we can apply the access functions to construct functions which manipulate trees. These higher level procedures will be independent of the way the access functions are implemented. The access functions can be treated as building bricks which can be used and reused to build hierarchies of software components (see Figure 5.4).

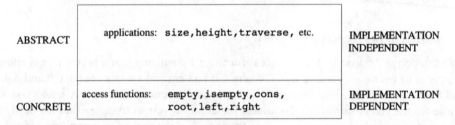

Figure 5.4

Example

Suppose that we want to use the access functions to write a function which takes a tree as a parameter and returns the number of data items it contains. We can specify the algorithm by case analysis: a tree is either empty or of the form (cons i l r), where i is a data item and l and r are trees. The first case is trivial:

```
size empty = 0
```

In the second case, we have

```
size (cons i l r) = 1 + (size l) + (size r)
```

The specification given above uses pattern matching; as the implementation of the ADT will be protected we must use the access functions instead. With this in mind, and adding the necessary syntactic sugar to translate the specification into SML, we get:

```
(*Pre: takes a tree
   Post: returns the number of nodes in the tree *)
 fun size t = if isempty t then 0
              else
                  1 + (size (left t)) + (size (right t))
```

Before we give some more examples, we will use the following section to introduce some more terminology.

DEFINITIONS

There is a large amount of nomenclature associated with trees; this section contains definitions of some of the most relevant terms.

- A *path* of a tree is a sequence of successive, distinct nodes of non-empty subtrees.
- The *level* of a node in a tree is 1 if the node is the root of the tree, otherwise it is one more than the level of its parent.

For example, Figure 5.5 shows the levels of all the nodes in a tree.

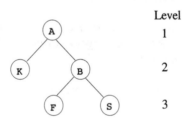

	Level
A	1
K B	2
F S	3

Figure 5.5

An important characteristic of a tree is its *height*:

- The *height* (or *depth*) of a tree is defined to be the maximum level of its nodes. An empty tree has a height of zero.

So, for example, the height of the tree in Figure 5.5 is 3.
   Similarly, we can also define the shortest path of a tree:

- The *shortest path* of a tree is defined to be the minimum level of its nodes. An empty tree has a shortest path of zero.

Thus the shortest path of the tree in Figure 5.5 is 2.

Example

From the definition of a tree's height we can derive (by case analysis) the following specification for a function which takes a tree as parameter and returns its height:

```
height empty = 0
height (cons i l r) = 1 + max2 (height l)  (height r)
```

where max2 is a library function which returns the maximum of two numbers. We can produce an SML function from this specification by using the access functions and adding the necessary syntax:

```
(*Post: returns the height of a tree *)
fun height t =  if isempty t then 0
                else
                1 + (max2 (height (left t)) (height (right t)))
```

EXERCISE 5.1

1. Write a function which takes a tree as parameter and returns its shortest path. The specification for the function is given below:

```
shortest empty = 0
shortest (cons i l r) = 1 +  min2 (shortest l)  (shortest r)
```

where min2 is a function which returns the minimum of two numbers.

All of the nodes shown in Figure 5.5 are *internal nodes*. The tree in Figure 5.6 has been extended by replacing every empty subtree by an *external node* (shown by a rectangle). This concept yields the following definition:

● The *external path length* of an extended binary tree is the sum of the levels of all external nodes.

For example, the external path length of the tree in Figure 5.6 is 22.

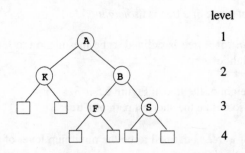

Figure 5.6 An extended binary tree

Similarly:

● The *internal path length* of a binary tree is the sum of levels of all the internal nodes.

For example, the internal path length of the tree in Figure 5.6 is 11.

An important characteristic of a tree is its shape. This is formalised by the following definition:

● A tree is said to be *perfectly balanced* (or *full*) if its height and its shortest path both have the same value.

We can see from this definition that a full binary tree has the maximum possible number of nodes. That is, all its internal nodes have two children and so its leaves are all at the same level (for example, see Figure 5.7).

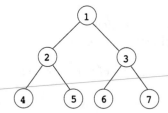

Figure 5.7 A full binary tree of height 3

The relationship between the number of nodes in a full binary tree and its height is given by the following theorem.

Theorem

The number of nodes in a perfectly balanced binary tree of height h ($h \geq 0$) is $2^h - 1$.

Proof

The proof is by induction on h.

First we must prove the theorem for $h = 0$.
If $h = 0$ the tree is empty. An empty tree is perfectly balanced, and since $2^0 - 1 = 0$, the result holds for $h = 0$. For the inductive hypothesis, we assume that, for some $k \geq 0$, a full binary tree of height k has

$2^k - 1$ nodes

Now a perfectly balanced tree of height $(k + 1)$ consists of a root and two subtrees which are both perfectly balanced trees of height k (by definition of a full tree). By the inductive hypothesis, the left subtree has $2^k - 1$ nodes and similarly for the right subtree. So the number of nodes in the tree is:

number of nodes in left subtree + number of nodes in right subtree + 1 (the root)

$= 2^k - 1 + 2^k - 1 + 1 = 2 * (2^k - 1) + 1$

$= 2^{k+1} - 1$

Therefore by induction the theorem is true for all h, that is, a full binary tree of height h has 2^h-1 nodes.

It follows that this is the maximum number of nodes that a binary tree of height h can have.

Corollary

A perfectly balanced tree with n nodes has a height of $h = \log_2(n+1)$.

We can relax the definition of perfect balance to give the following definition of *balance*:

- A tree is said to be *balanced* if the numbers of nodes in the left and right subtrees of every internal node do not differ by more than one.

Thus, although a full tree is an example of a balanced tree, a balanced tree is not necessarily full.

A *complete* tree is a balanced tree with an extra constraint on it:

- A *complete* tree of height h is a balanced tree that is full down to level $h-1$ with level h filled in from left to right.

Thus, a complete tree of height h has a total of 2^h-1 nodes in the first $(h-1)$ levels, and all non-empty leaves in level h are situated towards the left of the tree. For example, the tree in Figure 5.8(a) is a complete binary tree.

For a given number of nodes n, the tree which has the smallest height is a balanced tree, and this has height h where

$$\log_2 (n + 1) - 1 < h \leq \log_2 (n + 1)$$

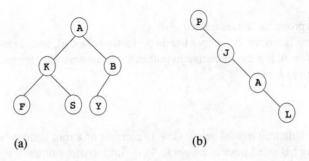

(a)   (b)

Figure 5.8 Two binary trees

Figure 5.8(b) shows an *imbalanced* tree (also called a *skewed, linear* or *degenerate* tree). It could be used to represent the ADT stack, since it is a linear sequence in which each node has at most one subtree.

The following section discusses the ways in which the nodes in a binary tree can be processed, using the access functions.

TREE TRAVERSAL

The process of visiting all the nodes in a tree is called tree *traversal*. There are three methods which may be used: *inorder*, *preorder* and *postorder*. For *inorder*, we visit the root *in between* visiting the subtrees. The left subtree is always visited first, then the root, and then the right subtree. For a *preorder* traversal, the root is visited *before* visiting the left subtree and then the right subtree in preorder. Finally, *postorder* traversal means visiting the left subtree and then the right subtree in postorder and then visiting the root after that.

Example

Visiting the nodes of the tree in Figure 5.9 in each of the three orders gives:

1. preorder   1 2 4 5 3 6 7
2. inorder   4 2 5 1 6 3 7
3. postorder   4 5 2 6 7 3 1

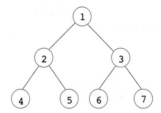

Figure 5.9

Using the descriptions of tree traversal given above we can develop a set of traversal functions. The functions will return a list of the nodes in the order in which they are visited. For example, we can derive an inorder traversal function by using case analysis as follows: if the tree t is empty then there is nothing to do and so the returned list is empty:

```
if isempty t then []
```

Otherwise, the tree has a left subtree, a root and a right subtree, which must be visited in that order. We can use the append function, @, to join together the sublists which are produced as the result:

```
(inorder (left t))@[root t]@ (inorder (right t))
```

Putting the cases together and adding some syntactic sugar gives us the function below:

```
(*Post: returns the result of traversing the tree in inorder *)
fun inorder t = if isempty t then []
                else
                (inorder (left t))@[root t]@ (inorder (right t))
```

If the tree contains an arithmetic expression then these methods of traversal will yield the expression written in prefix, infix and postfix notation. For example, the result of traversing the tree in Figure 5.10 in inorder gives us a conventional infix expression:

(A + B) * (C − D)   (1)

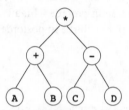

Figure 5.10

Traversing the tree in preorder gives us the prefix expression:

* + A B − C D

This is equivalent to expression (1) above. Similarly, traversing the tree in Figure 5.10 in postorder gives us the postfix expression below:

A B + C D − *

EXERCISES 5.2

1. Write a function which returns a list of the items of a tree in preorder

2. Write a function which returns a list of the items of a tree in postorder

3. Write down the result of traversing the tree in Figure 5.11 in inorder, preorder and postorder.

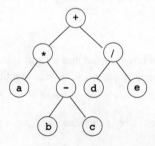

Figure 5.11

HIGHER ORDER FUNCTIONS

In the same way that we developed higher order functions for lists, we can also develop them for trees. For example, we may want to apply some function to every item in a tree;

if the items are integers, we may want to double every item, or triple it, or increment every item by one. This calls for a function which is analogous to the function map which we developed for lists. Its derivation is discussed below.

The Function maptree

This function takes any monadic function and a tree and returns a tree in which the function has been applied to each item of the tree in turn.

To derive the function, we will use case analysis. A tree is either empty or it has a root and two subtrees (which may of course be empty). If the tree, t, is empty then there is nothing to do:

```
if isempty t then empty
```

Otherwise, we apply the function (called f below) to the root of the tree:

```
f (root t)
```

and call the function again to deal with the nodes in the left subtree:

```
maptree f (left t)
```

and similarly for the right subtree. We then rebuild the tree using cons:

```
cons (f(root t)) (maptree f (left t)) (maptree f (right t))
```

Adding the necessary syntactic constructs gives us the executable function below:

```
(*Pre: takes a monadic function and a tree
   Post: applies the function to each item and returns the resulting
   tree *)
fun maptree f t = if isempty t then empty
                  else
                  cons (f(root t)) (maptree f (left t)) (maptree f
                                                         (right t))
```

For example, suppose we have the tree of integers shown in Figure 5.12.

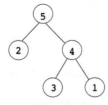

Figure 5.12

Following the notation introduced at the beginning of the chapter, we can represent this tree in the flattened form:

```
((2), 5,  ((3), 4,  (1)))
```

If we want to increment every value in the tree then we could use the ap function from
our library, together with the operator +. For example:

```
maptree (ap op+ 1) (cons 5 (cons 2 empty empty) (cons 4 (cons 3 empty
                                                               empty)
                                                 (cons 1 empty empty)))
```

The evaluation of this call to maptree is shown below, where the tree is represented
using its flattened form, rather than showing its construction using cons.

```
maptree (ap op+ 1) ((2), 5, ((3), 4, (1)))

→ cons (5+1) (maptree (ap op+ 1)(2)) (maptree (ap op+ 1)((3),4,
                                                               (1)))

→ cons (6 (cons (2+1)(maptree (ap op+ 1) empty)(maptree (ap op+ 1)
                                                               empty))
   (cons ((ap op+ 1)(4) (maptree (ap op+ 1) (3))(maptree (ap op+ 1)
                                                               (1)))))

→ cons 6 (cons 3 empty  empty ) (cons 5 (maptree (ap op+ 1) (3))
                                         (maptree (ap op+ 1)  (1)))

→ cons 6 (3) (cons 5 (cons (3+1) empty  empty) (cons (ap op+ 1)
                                         (1) empty  empty))

→ cons (6 (3) (cons (5 (4)(2)))))

→  ((3), 6, ((4), 5, (2)))
```

which is the flattened form of the tree in Figure 5.13.

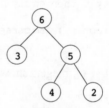

Figure 5.13

The Function foldtree

Similarly, we can write a higher order function foldtree which takes all the values in a
tree and reduces them to a single value.

There are several ways that we can do this. We will develop a version which folds up
the right subtree first. The function takes a dyadic function, f, a tree, t, and a base case b
which accumulates the result. The function can be derived by case analysis; a tree is
either empty or it consists of a root and two subtrees. If the tree is empty then we simply
return the base case:

```
if isempty t then b
```

Now suppose that the tree is not empty. We must apply the function f to the value at the root of the tree and the value we have obtained by applying the function foldtree to (say) the right subtree and the base case:

```
(f (root t) (foldtree f (right t) b))
```

We must also reduce the left subtree, using the value obtained by reducing the rest of the tree as the base case. This gives us:

```
foldtree f (left t) (f (root t) (foldtree f (right t) b))
```

Thus, the right subtree is reduced first, then the root, and finally the left subtree. Adding the necessary SML syntax gives us the executable function below:

```
(*Pre: takes a dyadic function, a tree and a base case
   Post: applies the function to the items in the tree, returning a
   single value *)
fun foldtree f t b = if isempty t then b
                     else
                         foldtree f (left t) (f (root t) (foldtree f
                                                         (right t) b))
```

For example, suppose that we wish to fold the tree of strings shown in Figure 5.14 using the function inc given below:

```
fun inc i j = j +1
```

Figure 5.14

Using a base case of zero, the evaluation proceeds as follows, where empty brackets, ( ), are used to denote an empty tree:

```
foldtree inc ((b), a, (d)) 0
    → foldtree inc (b) (inc a (foldtree inc (d) 0))
    → foldtree inc (b) (inc a (foldtree inc ( ) (inc d (foldtree inc
                                                        ( ) 0))))
    → foldtree inc (b) (inc a (foldtree inc ( ) (inc d 0)))
    → foldtree inc (b) (inc a (foldtree inc ( ) 1))
    → foldtree inc (b) (inc a 1)
    → foldtree inc (b) 2
    → foldtree inc ( ) (inc b (foldtree inc ( ) 2))
    → foldtree inc ( ) (inc b 2)
    → foldtree inc ( ) 3
    → 3
```

which is the number of items in the tree.

Another way to define `foldtree` is given below. This reduces the right subtree to a single value, then reduces the left subtree, using this value as the base case, and finally applies the dyadic function to the value at the root and the results of the reductions.

```
(*Pre: takes a dyadic function, a tree and a base case
   Post: applies the function to the items in the tree, returning a
   single value *)
fun foldtree f t b = if isempty t then b
                     else
                       f (root t) (foldtree f (left t) (foldtree f
                                                        (right t) b))
```

EXERCISES 5.3

1. Rewrite the following expression to normal form, using the second version of foldtree:

   ```
   foldtree inc ((b), a, (d)) 0
   ```

2. Assuming that the function f is triadic, write a symmetrical `foldtree` function by reducing both subtrees independently and then applying the reducing function to the results.

IMPLEMENTATION

We will now look at possible implementations for the ADT. We start by defining a signature for the items in the tree:

```
signature ITEM =
  sig
  eqtype item
  val isequal : item -> item -> bool
  (*Post: returns true if the items are equal *)
  val isless : item -> item -> bool
  (*Post: returns true if the 1st item is smaller than the 2nd *)
  val isgreater : item -> item -> bool
  (*Post: returns true if the 1st item is larger than the 2nd *)
  val showitem : item -> string
  (*Post: a display function which returns a string *)
  val format : string -> string list -> unit
  (*Post: opens a file and outputs a list of strings to it *)
  end
```

We will also define a signature for the ADT itself, which will be used as a constraint on the implementing functor:

```
signature TREE =
  sig
  structure I : ITEM
  type tree
  val empty : tree
```

```
        (*Post: returns an empty tree *)
        val isempty : tree -> bool
        (*Post: returns true if the tree is empty, otherwise false *)
        val cons : I.item -> tree -> tree -> tree
        (*Pre: takes an item and two trees
           Post: returns a new tree which has the given item at its root and
           the 2 trees as its left and right subtrees *)
        val left : tree -> tree
        (*Post : returns the left subtree of tree *)
        val right : tree -> tree
        (*Post : returns the right subtree of tree *)
        val root : tree -> I.item
        (*Post : returns the data item at the root of the tree  *)
        val showtree : tree -> string list
        (*Post: formats a tree for output to a text stream *)
        val show : tree -> string
        (*Post: formats a tree for output to the standard output stream *)
     end
```

In addition to the access functions specified earlier, we have included two display functions. The function show is a very simple display routine which can be used to send an instance of a tree to the standard output stream, whereas the function showtree can be used to send a fully formatted representation of a tree to a named output stream (examples of the use of these functions are given in the section on verification and validation).

We will implement the access functions using a functor called MkTree. The abstype declaration for the type constructor tree can mirror the definition of the ADT which we gave at the beginning of the chapter, which stated that a binary tree is either empty or consists of a data item and two disjoint binary trees. We can implement this by using an abstype declaration with two alternatives, one of which is defined by the data constructor Empty, and the other of which is defined by the data constructor Tree, by using the type constructor tree twice (for the left and right subtrees) and an element of type item. The functor heading and abstype declaration are given below:

```
functor MkTree (Itemstruct : ITEM) : TREE =
struct
structure I = Itemstruct    (*indicates that this item structure is the
                              same as that used in the signature*)

abstype tree = Empty | Tree of tree * I.item * tree
```

The constructor function empty can be implemented by using the data constructor Empty:

```
val empty = Empty
```

The predicate function isempty must only return true if its argument is the data constructor Empty:

```
fun isempty (Tree t) = false
  | isempty Empty = true
```

The second constructor function, cons, returns a tree, using its arguments as the subtrees and the root:

```
fun cons i l r = Tree (l,i,r)
```

The selector functions all return an error if called with an empty tree, according to the algebraic specification. Rather than leaving this to the system to cope with, we will incorporate these cases into the implementation of the functions by calling the function hd with an empty list. For non-empty trees, each selector function must return the appropriate part of the (l,i,r) tuple, yielding the following implementations:

```
fun left (Tree (l,i,r)) = l
  | left Empty = hd []

fun right (Tree (l,i,r)) = r
  | right Empty = hd []

fun root (Tree (l,i,r)) = i
  | root Empty = hd []
```

The function showtree formats trees as lists of strings (one per item) using the notation discussed in this chapter. It uses two other functions, showleft and showright, to ensure that commas are only inserted between items if a subtree is non-empty. Because of the mutual recursion involved here, we must use the keyword and, rather than fun, to declare the showleft and showright functions. The tree will be enclosed within brackets. The functions call showitem to convert the items to strings:

```
fun showtree (Tree (l,i,r)) = "("::(showleft l)@[I.showitem i]@
                                              (showright r) @ [")"]
  | showtree Empty = []

and showleft (Tree (l,i,r)) = showtree (Tree (l,i,r)) @ [","]
  | showleft Empty = []

and showright (Tree (l,i,r)) = "," :: (showtree (Tree (l,i,r)))
  | showright Empty = []
```

We also implemented a very basic display function for output to the standard output stream, which does not perform so much formatting, but simply returns a string:

```
fun show (Tree (l,i,r)) = "("^ show l ^(I.showitem i)^ show r ^ ")"
  | show Empty = ""
```

Verification and validation

As shown in previous chapters, we can both verify and validate the implementation of the access functions. The verification can proceed concurrently with the implementation, by rewriting calls to the access functions with an arbitrary instance of a tree, and checking the results against those predicted by the algebraic specification.

Before we validate the implementation, we must provide a structure to match the ITEM signature, such as the one for integers which is given below:

```
structure IntItem : ITEM =
  struct
    type item = int
    fun isequal a b = a = b
    fun isless (a:item) b = a < b
```

```
fun isgreater (a:item) b = a > b
fun showitem (a:item) = makestring a
fun format f xs = output (open_out f, showstring "tree " " "" "\n" xs)
(*Post: opens a file f and outputs the list of strings xs to f,
  using showstring to format the output *)
end
```

And we can now instantiate the MkTree functor by using this structure:

```
structure IntTree = MkTree (IntItem)
```

We can use this structure to test the access functions. For example, to find the left sub-tree of the tree in Figure 5.15, we could use an expression of the form:

```
show (left (cons 9 (cons 5 (cons 1 empty empty) (cons 6 empty empty))
                    (cons 15 (cons 12 empty empty) empty)))
```

which yields the answer:

```
"((1)5(6))" : string
```

agreeing with axiom 6 of the algebraic specification, which states that

```
left (cons i l r) = l.
```

Alternatively, to send the expression to a file, we can use an expression of the form:

```
format "f" (showtree (left (cons 9 (cons 5 (cons 1 empty empty)
                    (cons 6 empty empty)) (cons 15 (cons 12 empty empty)
                    empty)))))
```

which writes the following expression to the file f:

```
tree ((1),5,(6))
```

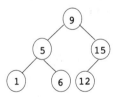

Figure 5.15

Applying the generic ADT

We can now implement the functions which we designed earlier in the chapter. To ensure that the code is well modularised we will define these functions within a functor which takes a structure of type TREE as a parameter. The applications functor could include any of the algorithms which were discussed earlier, but for the purpose of illustration we will only include the size and height functions.

```
functor MkApplications (structure T: TREE) =
struct

open T                            (* an alternative to using dot notation *)

(*Pre: takes a tree
  Post: returns the number of nodes in the tree *)
fun size t = if isempty t then 0
                else
                   1 + (size (left t)) + (size (right t))

(*Post: returns the height of a tree *)
fun height t =  if isempty t then 0
                else
                   1 + (max2 (height (left t)) (height (right t)))

end
```

We can instantiate this functor by using a tree structure such as the one we defined earlier:

```
structure IntApps = MkApplications (structure  T = IntTree)
```

Now, by opening the structure IntApps, we can find the height of the tree in Figure 5.15 by evaluating an expression of the form:

```
height (cons 9 (cons 5 (cons 1 empty empty) (cons 6 empty empty))
                           (cons 15 (cons 12 empty empty) empty))
```

to obtain the answer 3, and so on.

SUMMARY

- The ADT *binary tree* is a finite set of nodes which is either empty or consists of a data item (called the *root*) and two disjoint binary trees (called the *left* and *right subtrees* of the root) together with six access functions (empty, cons, isempty, root, left and right).
- A *path* of a tree is a sequence of successive, distinct nodes of non-empty subtrees.
- The *height* of a tree can be specified as follows:

```
height empty = 0
height (cons i l r) = 1 + max2 (height l) (height r)
```

- The *shortest path* of a tree can be defined as follows:

```
shortest empty = 0
shortest (cons i l r) = 1 +  min2 (shortest l) (shortest r)
```

- A tree is *balanced* if the numbers of nodes in the left and right subtrees of every internal node do not differ by more than one.

- A tree is said to be *perfectly balanced* (or *full*) if its height and its shortest path both have the same value.
- The *level* of a node is 1 if the node is the root of the tree, otherwise it is defined to be one more than the level of its parent.
- A *complete* tree of height h is a tree that is full down to level $h-1$ with level h filled in from left to right.
- There are three methods which can be used to traverse a tree: *inorder*, *preorder* and *postorder*. For a tree containing an arithmetic expression, these orders correspond to infix, prefix and postfix notation respectively.
- As with all ADTs, since the implementation details are hidden the user will be unaware of the implementation, and so will be forced to use the access functions to manipulate the tree. This guarantees the behaviour and integrity of the ADT.

CHAPTER 6

Ordered Binary Trees

INTRODUCTION

This chapter deals with binary trees which have some sort of ordering imposed on the values which they contain. We start with a very useful form of tree called an *ordered binary tree,* or *binary search tree* (sometimes abbreviated to *search tree*). Because the values in this tree are ordered, it can be used for sorting and searching data, yielding particularly efficient algorithms. We give a more formal definition of ordered trees below, and then discuss their algebraic specification and demonstrate some examples of their use, before going on to develop a possible implementation. In this chapter we also demonstrate the reuse of ADTs, showing how priority queues can be implemented using ordered trees.

We also discuss an ordered tree called a *heap*, and another method of sorting which is very efficient called a *heapsort*. Finally, a more general method of maintaining the balance of binary trees is discussed.

DEFINITION

The ADT *ordered tree* is a binary tree in which the values in the nodes are ordered, together with a number of access functions. The ordering imposed on the nodes is such that, for each node, all values in its left subtree are less than the value in that node, and all values in its right subtree are greater than the value in that node.

Because we want to produce generally applicable, reusable software, we will assume that the values in the nodes of the tree can be of any type. However, the definition given above does assume that the values in the tree will be unique.

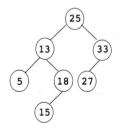

Figure 6.1 An ordered tree

If the values in the nodes are numbers then the ordering imposed on the values will be numerical: for example, Figure 6.1 shows an ordered tree of integers.

ALGEBRAIC SPECIFICATION

The algebraic specification of an ordered tree is very similar to that of a binary tree. The main difference is that the function cons should no longer be visible to the user of the ADT since it can be used to create unordered trees. Instead we will need a function which takes an item and an ordered tree and returns an ordered tree with the item inserted in the correct position:

```
val insert : item -> tree -> tree
(*Pre: takes an item and an ordered binary tree
  Post: returns an ordered binary tree with the given item inserted
  in the correct position *)
```

and we also need axioms to describe the semantics of this function. In order to produce trees without duplicate items, an item will only be inserted if it is not already in the tree. We can specify the function by case analysis, using the access functions for the ADT binary tree. The following assumes that i and j are of type item, whereas l and r are trees.

```
insert i empty = (cons i empty empty)

 insert i (cons j l r) = if i = j then
                             (cons j l r)
                         else
                         if i < j then
                                 (cons j (insert  i l ) r )
                         else
                         (cons j l (insert  i r ))
```

Another access function which we may find that we need is one which we can use to remove an item from the tree whilst maintaining the ordering of the items in the tree. We give the algebraic specification of the function below, using case analysis.

The function remove will take an item and an ordered tree and return an ordered tree without the specified item.

```
val remove : item -> tree -> tree
(*Pre: takes an item and an ordered binary tree
  Post: returns an ordered binary tree without the given item *)
```

If the tree is empty, then we will return an empty tree:

```
remove i empty = empty
```

If we find the item to be deleted at the root of the tree and the right subtree is empty, then we return the left subtree:

```
remove i (cons i l empty) = l
```

Similarly, if the item is at the root of the tree and the left subtree is empty, we return the right subtree:

```
remove i (cons i empty  r) = r
```

If neither subtree is empty, we must find some item to take the place of the item at the root. In doing so, we must ensure that the tree remains ordered. It can be seen by inspection that there are two items which are candidates for the replacement: the largest item in the tree's left subtree, and the smallest item in the right subtree. The latter is referred to as the root's *inorder successor*, as it is the item which succeeds the root when the tree is traversed in inorder. This is the item which we have (arbitrarily) decided to use. So we will replace the item at the root by the minimum item in the right subtree and remove this value from the right subtree:

```
remove i (cons i l r) = cons (min r) l (remove (min r) r )
```

where the function min returns the minimum item in an ordered tree.

If the item to be removed is not at the root, then we remove it from whichever subtree contains it:

```
remove i (cons j l r) = if i < j then (cons j (remove i l) r)
                        else
                        (cons j l (remove i r ))
```

Collecting these cases together gives us a specification in pseudocode for the function:

```
remove i empty = empty
remove i (cons i l empty) = l
remove i (cons i empty r) = r
remove i (cons i l r) = cons (min r) l (remove (min r) r )
remove i (cons j l r) = if i < j then (cons j (remove i l) r)
                        else
                        (cons j l (remove i r ))
```

Let us return to the function min. Because of the way in which the items are ordered in the tree, the smallest item in a non-empty ordered tree is always the item furthest to the left on the lowest level. Consequently, we can give the specification of this function as shown below:

```
val min : tree -> item
(*Pre: takes an ordered binary tree
  Post: returns the smallest item in the tree *)

min (cons i l r) = if isempty l then i else min l
```

Similarly, the largest item in a non-empty ordered tree is the one furthest to the right on the lowest level, and we can specify a function to find this item as:

```
val max : tree -> item
(*Pre: takes an ordered binary tree
```

```
Post: returns the largest item in the tree *)

max (cons i l r) = if isempty r then i else max r
```

We can now go on to construct functions which depend on the access functions.

APPLICATIONS

Ordered trees form an important subclass of the binary trees because of the efficient sorting and searching algorithms which can be implemented using them. A value can be located by traversing the tree, taking either the left or right subtree, depending on whether the value being sought is less than or greater than the value at the current root.

The hierarchy of software components can be viewed as shown in Figure 6.2, which shows how the binary tree access functions are used as the foundations of the system created to manipulate ordered trees.

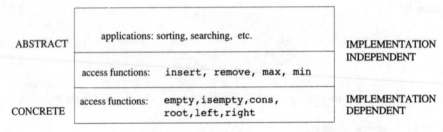

	applications: sorting, searching, etc.	
ABSTRACT		IMPLEMENTATION INDEPENDENT
	access functions: insert, remove, max, min	
CONCRETE	access functions: empty,isempty,cons, root,left,right	IMPLEMENTATION DEPENDENT

Figure 6.2

Theorem

In the worst case, the number of comparisons needed to find a particular value held in an ordered tree with n nodes is less than or equal to $\log_2(n+1)$, if the tree is balanced.

This follows from the fact (discussed in Chapter 5) that the height of a balanced tree is less than or equal to $\log_2(n+1)$, and since we always know which path to traverse we never need to backtrack.

The following section shows how ordered trees can be used for sorting.

Sorting

Using the access functions for the ordered tree ADT we can develop an efficient function to sort a set of items, by constructing an ordered tree from the given items and then traversing it in the correct order. Since the values in the nodes of the left subtree are less than the value at the root, whereas those in the right subtree are greater than it, the tree should be traversed using an inorder traversal function.

We will assume that the items to be sorted are stored in a list called **xs**. We can implement the sorting function, **treesort**, by using two auxiliary functions:

```
(*Pre: takes a list of items
   Post: returns a sorted list of items *)
fun treesort xs = inorder (build xs)
```

where build is a function which constructs an ordered tree and inorder performs an inorder traversal of it. Alternatively, we could implement treesort by composing the two functions together, using the composition operator o:

```
fun treesort xs = (inorder o build) xs
```

The function insert can be used to build an ordered tree by inserting the items one at a time into an ordered tree. Thus (using case analysis on the list) we can write the function build as:

```
(*Pre: takes a list of items
   Post: returns an ordered tree *)
fun build [] = empty
  | build (x::xs) = insert x (build xs)
```

For example, if the items to be sorted are given by the list [7,1,~5,9,3,6,4,~2,8], the function build will construct the tree shown in Figure 6.3 (note that the last item in the list is the first to be inserted in the tree). Traversing this tree in inorder then gives us the sorted list [~5,~2,1,3,4,6,7,8,9].

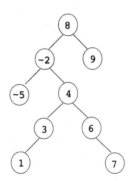

Figure 6.3

An asymptotic analysis of treesort shows that it requires $O(n\log_2 n)$ comparisons in the average case, but degenerates to $O(n^2)$ in the worst case (which happens if the tree is skewed so that it has a linear structure).

EXERCISE 6.1

1. Change the function build so that it uses an accumulating parameter which is initially an empty tree. How will this alteration affect the operation of treesort?

IMPLEMENTATION

We now turn to consider a possible implementation of the ordered tree ADT. As usual, we will start by giving a signature for the items in the tree.

```
signature ITEM =
  sig
  eqtype item
  val isequal : item -> item -> bool
  (*Post: returns true if the items are equal *)
  val isless : item -> item -> bool
  (*Post: returns true if the 1st item is smaller than the 2nd *)
  val isgreater : item -> item -> bool
  (*Post: returns true if the 1st item is larger than the 2nd *)
  val showitem : item -> string
  (*Post: a display function which returns a string *)
  val format : string -> string list -> unit
  (*Post: opens a file and outputs a list of strings to it *)
  val incfreq : item -> item
  (*Post:  increments the frequency fields of an item, if there is
    one, otherwise has no effect *)
  end
```

We suggested earlier that the items in an ordered tree should be unique. However, for generality, the signature for items includes a function, incfreq, which can be used if the values have frequencies associated with them, so that the frequency can be incremented if a value is inserted which is the same as an existing value in the tree. The existence of this function necessitates a change to the semantics of insert, the specification of which now becomes:

```
insert i empty = (cons i empty empty)
insert i (cons j l r) = if i = j then
                          (cons (incfreq j) l r)
                        else
                        if i < j then
                            (cons j (insert  i l ) r )
                        else (cons j l (insert  i r ))
```

We will also define a signature for the ordered tree ADT. This signature is the same as that of the tree ADT given in Chapter 5, except for the fact that cons is no longer available, and has been replaced by insert, and the functions remove, max and min are also provided.

```
signature TREE =
  sig
  structure I : ITEM
  type tree
  val empty : tree
  (*Post: returns an empty tree *)
  val isempty : tree -> bool
  (*Post: returns true if the tree is empty, otherwise false *)
  val insert : I.item -> tree -> tree
  (*Pre: takes an item and an ordered binary tree
```

```
        Post: returns an ordered binary tree with the given item inserted
        in the correct position *)
      val left : tree -> tree
      (*Post : returns the left subtree of tree *)
      val right : tree -> tree
      (*Post : returns the right subtree of tree *)
      val root : tree -> I.item
      (*Post : returns the data item at the root of the tree  *)
      val remove : I.item -> tree -> tree
      (*Pre: takes an item and an ordered binary tree
        Post: returns an ordered binary tree without the given item *)
      val max : tree -> I.item
      (*Pre: takes an ordered binary tree
        Post: returns the largest item in the tree *)
      val min : tree -> I.item
      (*Pre: takes an ordered binary tree
        Post: returns the smallest item in the tree *)
      val showtree : tree -> string list
      (*Post: formats a tree for output to a text stream *)
      val show : tree -> string
      (*Post: formats a tree for output to the standard output stream *)
    end
```

We will declare a functor called MkOrdTree and use the same implementation for the ordered tree abstype as the one we gave for the tree ADT:

```
functor MkOrdTree (Itemstruct : ITEM) : TREE =
struct
structure I = Itemstruct    (*indicates that this item structure is the
                              same as that used in the signature*)

abstype tree = Empty | Tree of tree * I.item * tree
```

The access functions which are the same as those given for binary trees can be implemented in exactly the same way, and so in this section we will only consider the functions insert, remove, max and min.

We will implement the insert function by considering the algebraic specification. We can use the function cons on the right hand side of the equations, and implement the specification almost directly:

```
fun insert i Empty = cons i empty empty
  | insert i (Tree (l,j,r))
                  = if I.isequal i j then cons (I.incfreq j) l r
                    else
                    if I.isless i j then cons j (insert i l) r
                    else
                    cons j l (insert i r)
```

We can also translate the specification of the function remove into SML by using the access functions for the tree ADT:

```
fun remove i t = if isempty t then t
                 else
```

```
if I.isequal i (root t) then
    if isempty (left t) then (right t)
    else
    if isempty (right t) then (left t)
    else
    cons (min (right t)) (left t) (remove (min
                                   (right t)) (right t))
else
if I.isless i (root t) then
cons (root t) (remove i (left t)) (right t)
else
cons (root t) (left t) (remove i (right t))
```

The functions min and max are very similar to each other, and can also be implemented by considering the specifications which were given earlier. For example, for the function min we have:

```
fun min t = if isempty (left t) then root t
            else min (left t)
```

We have included the functions min and max as access functions in the implementing functor (rather than in an applications functor) partly because min is used by the function remove and partly because they help to define the behaviour of the ADT, and may well be of use to other systems which can be constructed using this ADT.

Validation

To validate the implementation, we will provide a simple structure which implements the ITEM signature, such as the structure given below, in which the items are integers:

```
structure IntItem : ITEM =
  struct
  type item = int
  fun isequal a b = a = b
  fun isless (a:item) b = a < b
  fun isgreater (a:item) b = a > b
  fun showitem (a:item) = makestring a
  fun format f xs = output (open_out f, showstring "tree " "" "\n" xs)
  (*Post: opens a file f and outputs the list of strings xs to f,
     using showstring to format the output *)
  fun incfreq a = a
  end
```

Here, the function incfreq is given as the identity function, because the items do not have an associated frequency field.

We can now create ordered trees of integers by passing the IntItem structure to the functor MkOrdTree:

```
structure IntOrdTree = MkOrdTree (IntItem)
```

This structure can be used to validate the access functions, using the algebraic specification as an oracle.

As a second example, if the items in the ordered tree are strings with associated frequency fields then the item structure could be of the form given below:

```
structure  StringItem : ITEM =
  struct
  type item = (string * int)
  fun isequal   (s1,i) (s2,j) = s1 = s2
  fun isless (s1:string,i) (s2,j) = s1 < s2
  fun isgreater (s1:string,i) (s2,j) = s1 > s2
  fun showitem  (s,i:int) = "<" ^ s ^ "," ^ makestring i ^ ">"
  fun format f xs = output (open_out f, showstring "tree " " " "\n" xs)
  (*Post: opens a file f and outputs the list of strings xs to f,
     using showstring to format the output *)
  fun incfreq (s1,i) = (s1,i+1)
  end
```

Using this structure we can create ordered trees of this type by passing this structure as a parameter to the MkOrdTree functor:

```
structure StringOrdTree = MkOrdTree (StringItem)
```

We can then create trees which contain items of this type. For example:

```
format "f1" (showtree (insert ("sml",1) (insert ("hope",1)
      (insert ("sasl",1) (insert ("krc",1) (insert ("krc",1)
      (insert ("hope",1) (insert ("orwell", 1) empty)))))))))
```

sends the following expression to the file f1:

```
tree ((<hope,2>,(<krc,2>)),<orwell,1>,(<sasl,1>,(<sml,1>)))
```

which is the flattened form of the tree shown in Figure 6.4.

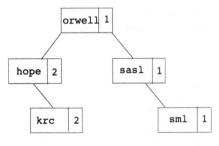

Figure 6.4

Applying the ADT

Sorting

As usual, we will collect the applications which use the access functions (such as the treesort function) together in a functor. The structures over which the functor is parametrised depend on the functions which are used within the functor. If functions from structures with signature ITEM are used as well as from structures with the signature TREE, then a typical application functor may have the heading shown below:

```
functor MkApplications (structure I : ITEM and T: TREE) =
  struct
```

etc.

Suppose that we need to produce a function which accepts a list of words, some of which may be repeated, and returns the list sorted into alphabetical order, together with a count of the number of occurrences of each word. (This is sometimes called the *concordance* problem.)

We can use the StringOrdTree structure created earlier and the treesort function to solve this problem. For example, if we evaluate the following expression:

```
treesort [("sml",1),("hope",1),("sasl",1),("krc",1),("krc",1),
                        ("hope",1),("orwell",1)]
```

an intermediate tree structure will be constructed (the tree shown in Figure 6.4), and after treesort has called the inorder function, we obtain the resulting sorted list of items:

```
[("hope",2),("krc",2),("orwell",1),("sasl",1),("sml",1)] : item list
```

Searching

Now suppose that we would like to implement ordered trees in which each item has a search key. This may be of use, for example, if the data to be stored in the tree is in the form of a large data structure, such as a tuple containing personal information of employees (a name, address, salary, age, etc.). Such information may well be tagged by a number (a *search key*) which can be used to retrieve the information quickly.

We will need to implement a new structure to match the ITEM signature, in which the items' search keys (rather than their data) are compared for equality, and so on. For example, if we call this structure TaggedItem, we could give the following structure heading, type declaration and comparison functions:

```
structure  TaggedItem : ITEM =
  struct
  type item = (string * int)
  fun isequal  (s1,i) (s2,j) = i = j
  (*Post: returns true if the items' keys are equal *)
  fun isless (s1,i:int) (s2,j) = i < j
  (*Post: returns true if the first key is less than the second *)
  fun isgreater (s1,i:int) (s2,j) = i > j
  (*Post: returns true if the first key is greater than the second *)
```

etc.

We will need to add some extra comparison functions to this structure (and the corresponding type information to the relevant signature). These functions will take an item and an integer key and compare the two. For example:

```
val isequalkey : item -> int -> bool
(*Pre: takes an item and an integer
  Post: returns true if the item's key is the same as the given
  integer *)

fun isequalkey (sl,i:int) j = i = j
```

To find out whether or not an item with a particular search key is in the tree or not, we will need a function which takes an ordered tree and an integer (a search key) and returns true if the item with the given key is in the tree and false if it is not. This function is given below:

```
(*Pre: takes a tree and an integer key
  Post: returns true if the item with the given key is in the tree,
  otherwise false *)
fun isin t i =  if isempty t then false
                else
                if I.isequalkey (root t) i then true
                else
                if I.islesskey (root t) i then
                  (*the key at the root is < the key which is sought *)
                    isin (right t) i
                else
                isin (left t) i
```

Having checked that the item being sought is in the tree, to actually retrieve the information which is associated with a particular key we can use the function find, given below:

```
(*Pre: takes a tree and an integer key
  Post: returns the data associated with the given key  *)
fun find t i = if I.isequalkey (root t) i then root t
               else
               if I.islesskey (root t) i then find (right t) i
               else
               find (left t) i
```

For example, suppose that we wanted to find the data which is associated with the key 145 in the tree shown in Figure 6.5 (in which the data has been abbreviated to a name). The tree is given by the value declaration shown below:

```
val tl = insert ("ann",197) (insert ("fay",165)  (insert ("sarah",145)
            (insert ("ken",121) (insert ("pat",131)
            (insert ("john",184) (insert ("ros", 152) empty))))))
```

To find the data we would use an expression of the following form:

```
find  tl 145
```

and the item retrieved from the tree would be:

```
> ("sarah",145) : item
```

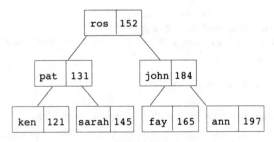

Figure 6.5

The efficiency of this searching algorithm is $O(\log_2 n)$, for a tree of n items, provided that the tree is balanced.

EXERCISES 6.2

1. Prove that the function `treesort` produces an ordered list of items. (Hint: use structural induction.)

2. Prove that the minimum height h of a tree with n nodes is such that:

$$\log_2 (n + 1) - 1 < h \le \log_2 (n + 1)$$

REUSING ADTs TO CONSTRUCT ADTs

In this section we demonstrate how ADTs can be reused to build hierarchies of software components.

We discussed the ADT queue earlier in the book, and one variation of it, the *priority queue*. This is a queue in which each item has an associated priority. Items are removed from the front of the queue, but must be inserted in such a way as to maintain the ordering of items in the queue. If a priority queue is implemented as shown in Chapter 4 (using a list), then inserting a new item may, in the worst case, involve traversing the entire list. The efficiency of insertion is therefore $O(n)$ where n is the number of items in the queue.

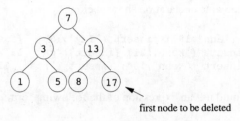

first node to be deleted

Figure 6.6 An ordered tree

Alternatively, we could consider using an ordered tree to implement a priority queue. To insert an item we first have to search the tree to find where it should be placed. If the tree is balanced and there are n items in the tree this means inspecting, at most, $O(\log_2 n)$ items, since this is the height of the tree. Finding the item at the front of the queue means finding the item which is furthest right in the tree, again involving $O(\log_2 n)$ indirections if the tree is balanced (see Figure 6.6). So although this implementation does not give any improvement for deletion over the list implementation it may do for insertion.

Turning to the implementation, we can reuse the ordered tree implementation by creating a functor for priority queues which is parameterised over items and trees. We have to inform the system that the items in the trees and those in the priority queues are the same; this is done by a *sharing constraint* in the functor heading. For example, a possible functor heading for priority queues is shown below:

```
functor MkPriorityQ (structure I: ITEM
                     and T : TREE
                     sharing type I.item = T.I.item ) : PRIORITYQ =
struct
structure I = I
```

etc.

Note that the line:

```
structure I = I
```

is needed because the priority queue signature (which was given in Chapter 4) specifies the use of such a structure.

Within this functor we can implement the priority queue ADT as a tree by using the statement:

```
abstype priorityq = PriorityQ of T.tree
```

The access functions given in the priority queue signature can now be implemented, using those provided for trees. For example:

```
val empty = PriorityQ T.empty
```

Here, `T.empty` accesses the function `empty` within the structure `T` with signature `TREE`. Similarly, for the other access functions, we have:

```
fun isempty (PriorityQ qs) = T.isempty qs

fun front (PriorityQ qs) = if T.isempty qs then hd []
                                                    (*generate an error*)
                           else T.max qs

fun back (PriorityQ qs) = if T.isempty qs then
                              PriorityQ (T.left qs)
                                                    (*generate an error*)
                          else PriorityQ (T.remove (T.max qs) qs)

fun insert i (PriorityQ qs) = PriorityQ (T.insert i qs)
```

The type of the items in the queue can be instantiated in the usual way. For example, we could declare a structure (called `StringIntItem`, say) in which the items in the queues consist of (string, integer) pairs (where the integers represent the priorities attached to the strings), as shown below.

```
structure StringIntItem : ITEM =
  struct
  type item = (string * int)
  fun isequal (s1,i:int) (s2,j) = i = j
  (*Post: returns true if the item's priorities are equal *)
  fun isless (s1,i:int) (s2,j) = i < j
  (*Post: returns true if the first item's priority is less than the
     second 's*)
  fun isgreater (s1,i:int) (s2,j) = i > j
  (*Post: returns true if the first item's priority is greater than
     the second 's*)
  fun showitem  (s,i:int) = "(" ^ s ^ "," ^ makestring i ^ ")"
  (*Post: a display function which returns a string *)
  fun format f xs = output (open_out f, showstring "queue{" " " "}\n"
                                                                  xs)
  (*Post: opens a file f and outputs the list of strings xs to f,
     using showstring to format the output *)
  fun incfreq  (s,i:int) =  (s,i:int)
  (*Post: an identity function, provided for compatibility only *)
  end
```

We can now form an ordered tree of this type, by passing `StringIntItem` as a parameter to the `MkOrdTree` functor:

```
structure StringIntTree = MkOrdTree  (StringIntItem)
```

and we can also create a priority queue using this type by passing the structures `StringIntItem` and `StringIntTree` to the `MkPriorityQ` functor:

```
structure StringPriorityQ = MkPriorityQ (structure I = StringIntItem
                                                 and T = StringIntTree)
```

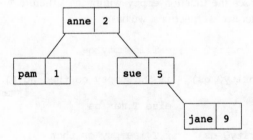

Figure 6.7

If we now open the `StringIntItem` and `StringPriorityQ` structures, we can evaluate an expression of the form:

```
insert ("jane",9) (insert ("pam",1) (insert ("sue",5) (insert ("anne",
                                                            2) empty)))
```

which corresponds to the tree in Figure 6.7.

Thus we have created a system for manipulating priority queues by reusing the ordered tree ADT.

REUSING ADTs TO CONSTRUCT APPLICATIONS

One of the problems caused by implementing priority queues using ordered binary trees is that the efficiency of insertion depends on the height of the tree, and unfortunately we cannot rely on an ordered tree remaining balanced. We will now discuss a tree called a *heap* which can be constructed by reusing the binary tree ADT, and which is guaranteed to remain balanced. The operations that we need to perform on a heap to keep it balanced are relatively simple compared with trying to maintain the balance of an ordered tree. We will then discuss two applications of heaps: an extremely efficient sorting algorithm called *heapsort,* and the implementation of priority queues.

Heaps

Definition

A *heap* is a complete binary tree which has an ordering imposed on the values in its nodes such that the value at the root of the tree is greater than or equal to the values of both of its children, and both subtrees are also heaps.

In the following section we specify the functions which we will need to construct heaps before going on to show how to implement them. We will assume that our system will be built by reusing the implementation of the binary tree ADT given in Chapter 5, and that we have access to any functions which have already been developed using the access functions for binary trees.

Specification

The definition of a *complete* binary tree of height h, given in Chapter 5, stated that it is a tree which is full down to level $h - 1$ with level h filled in from left to right. For example, the tree in Figure 6.8 is complete. The numbers 1 to 6 indicate the order in which the items were inserted into the tree.

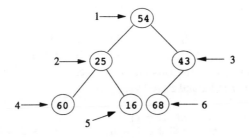

Figure 6.8

In order to construct a complete tree we will create a tree which is full down to its last level but one, and is filled from left to right on the lowest level. So we need a predicate function which can be used to determine whether or not a tree is full. From the specification of a full tree, we know that a tree is full if it is empty or if the heights of its left and right subtrees are the same and they are both full. This gives us the following pseudocode:

```
val isfull : tree -> bool
(*Post: returns true if the tree is full, otherwise false *)

isfull empty = true
isfull (cons i l r) = if  height l = height r
                           and isfull l and isfull r then true
                      else false
```

It is possible for a heap to be empty (since an empty tree is complete). Figure 6.9 shows a heap of eight items.

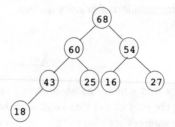

Figure 6.9 A heap of eight items

We will also need a function which can be used to insert an item into a complete binary tree in such a way that the resulting tree is complete. The function heading is given below:

```
val insert : item -> tree -> tree
(*Pre: takes an item and a complete binary tree
  Post: returns a complete binary tree *)
```

We can specify this function by case analysis. A tree is either empty or has been constructed (using cons) from an item and two subtrees. If the tree is empty, then we simply form a tree with the item i at the root and two empty subtrees:

```
insert i empty = cons i  empty empty
```

There are two situations in which we would insert an item into the left subtree: if the tree is full, or if the height of the left subtree is one greater than the height of the right and the left subtree is not full. Using this analysis gives us the following specification, in which i and j are items and l and r are trees:

```
insert i (cons j l r) = if isfull l or
                          height l = height r +1 and not isfull l then
                             cons j (insert i l) r
```

otherwise, we insert the item into the right subtree:

```
else cons j  r (insert  i l)
```

Using the function `insert`, we can specify a function which takes a list and an empty tree and returns a complete tree. The function heading is as follows:

```
val mkcomplete :  item list -> tree -> tree
(*Pre: the tree is empty initially
  Post: returns a complete tree containing the items in the list  *)
```

We will specify the function by using case analysis over the list, inserting the items one at a time into the given tree:

```
mkcomplete [] t = t
mkcomplete (x::xs) t = mkcomplete xs (insert x t)
```

A heap is not only a complete tree; it also has an ordering constraint on the values in its nodes. Consequently we will need a function which takes a complete tree and (possibly after rearranging the values in it) returns a heap:

```
val buildheap : tree -> tree
(*Pre: takes a complete binary tree
  Post: returns a heap *)
```

In order to specify this function, we will assume the existence of a function called `mkheap`, which takes an item and two trees which are heaps of the correct height (that is, the height of the tree which will form the left subtree is either the same as that of the right subtree, or one greater than it) and returns a heap. The pre- and postconditions for this function are given below:

```
val mkheap :  item  -> tree -> tree -> tree
(*Pre: takes an item and two heaps which are such that
  0 <= height l - height r <= 1, where l = 1st heap, r = 2nd heap
  Post: returns a heap *)
```

The function `buildheap`, which will call this function, will check that the heights of the two trees satisfy the constraint given in the heading of `mkheap`, and call itself for each subtree before calling `mkheap`:

```
buildheap empty = empty
buildheap (cons i l r) = if height l - height r <= 1
                            and height l - height r >= 0 then
                            mkheap i (buildheap l) (buildheap r)
                         else error
```

We will also specify the function `mkheap` by using case analysis. First, if the left subtree (i.e. the first parameter of type `tree`) is empty, then the right must be as well, because of the height constraint. So in this case we can simply return a tree with the item `i` at the root and two empty subtrees:

```
mkheap  i empty r =  cons  i empty r
```

If the left subtree is not empty but the right is, then we must check the item to determine whether it is greater than the root of the left subtree, in which case we return the tree with the item i at its root. Otherwise we insert i into the left subtree of the left subtree (which must be empty because of the height constraint):

```
mkheap  i l empty = if i ≥ root l then
                         cons i l empty
                    else
                    cons (root l )  (cons i  empty empty) empty
```

If the left and the right subtrees are both non-empty, there are three possibilities: if the item i is greater than the items at the roots of both the subtrees then we can return the tree which is formed by placing i at the root and using the two subtrees as left and right subtrees:

```
mkheap  i l r  = if i ≥ (root l) and (i ≥ root r) then (cons i l r )
```

Otherwise, if the item at the root of the left subtree is greater than that at the root of the right, we form a tree with the root of the left subtree as the root, a left subtree which is formed by calling mkheap with i and the two subtrees of the left subtree, and the right subtree:

```
else
if root l ≥ root r then
     cons (root l) (mkheap i (left  l)  (right  l))  r
```

Otherwise, we do the same but with the root and subtrees of the right subtree:

```
else
cons (root r) l  (mkheap (i (left  r) (right  r)))
```

Implementation

The system which we have specified in the preceding section can be implemented by reusing the system created in Chapter 5 to manipulate the ADT binary tree. Consequently, the signatures for the items in the tree and for the binary tree itself will be taken to be the same as those given previously, called ITEM and TREE respectively. We will also assume that we have implemented a functor of applications, similar to the one discussed in Chapter 5. In addition, we will impose a signature constraint on this applications functor, to act as an interface for the applications. A possible signature for such a functor is given below:

```
signature APPS =
  sig
  structure I : ITEM
  structure T : TREE
  open I
  open T
```

```
     val size : tree -> int
     (*Post: returns the size of the given tree *)
     val height : tree -> int
     (*Post: returns the height of the given tree *)
     val shortest : tree -> int
     (*Post: returns the length of the shortest path through the given
        tree *)
     val inorder : tree -> item list
     (*Post: returns the result of traversing the given tree in inorder *)
   end
```

A functor partially implementing this signature is given below (only the function height is shown in the body, as the others were discussed in Chapter 5). Note that the line:

```
structure T = T
```

is necessary because the constraint signature, APPS, specifies the existence of such a structure. As the postconditions were included in the constraining signature, they are not included in the functor.

```
functor MkApplications (structure T: TREE) : APPS =
struct
structure T = T

open T

fun height t =  if isempty t then 0
                else
                1 + (max2 (height(left t)) (height(right t)))

(*remaining body of functor ... *)

end
```

To ensure that the heap manipulation system which we are constructing is well-modularised, we will also encapsulate the access functions for heaps within a functor which is constrained by a signature such as the one shown below:

```
signature HEAP =
  sig
  structure I : ITEM
  structure T : TREE
  open I
  open T
  val isfull : tree -> bool
  (*Post: returns true if the tree is full, otherwise false *)
  val insert : item -> tree -> tree
  (*Pre: takes an item and a complete binary tree
    Post: returns a complete binary tree *)
  val mkcomplete :  item list -> tree -> tree
  (*Pre: the tree is empty initially
    Post: returns a complete tree containing the items in the list  *)
```

```
val mkheap :  item -> tree -> tree -> tree
(*Pre: takes an item and two heaps which are such that
   0 <= height l - height r <= 1, where l = 1st heap, r = 2nd heap
   Post: returns a heap *)
val buildheap : tree -> tree
(*Pre: takes a complete binary tree
   Post: returns a heap *)
end
```

The functor which is constrained by this signature is given below. Each function has been implemented directly from the specification given in the preceding section.

```
functor MkHeap (structure I : ITEM and T: TREE and A:APPS) : HEAP =
struct

open A          (*makes the functions declared within the applications
                   functor available *)
open T          (*makes the tree access functions available *)

fun isfull t = if isempty t then true
               else
               if (height (left t)) = (height (right t)) andalso
                      isfull (left t) andalso isfull (right t) then true
               else false

fun insert i t = if isempty t then cons i empty empty
                 else
                 if isfull t
                    orelse ((height (left t) = height (right t) + 1)
                    andalso not (isfull (left t))) then
                    cons (root t) (insert i (left t)) (right t)
                 else cons (root t) (left t) (insert i (right t))

fun mkcomplete [] t = t
  | mkcomplete (x::xs) t = mkcomplete xs (insert x t)

fun mkheap i l r = if isempty l then cons i l r
                   else
                   if isempty r then
                      if I.isgreater i (root l) then cons i l r
                      else cons (root l) (cons i empty empty) r
                   else
                   if (I.isgreater i (root l))
                      andalso (I.isgreater i (root r)) then
                      cons i l r
                   else
                   if I.isgreater (root l) (root r) then
                      cons (root l) (mkheap i (left l) (right l)) r
                   else cons (root r) l (mkheap i (left r) (right r))

fun buildheap t = if isempty t then t
                  else
                  if height (left t) - height (right t) <= 1 andalso
                        height (left t) - height (right t) >= 0 then
```

```
                    mkheap (root t) (buildheap (left t)) (buildheap
                                                            (right t))
           else left (empty)              (*generate an error *)
```

end

Before instantiating this functor, we must instantiate those on which it depends. For example, for heaps of integers, we could reuse the IntItem structure given in Chapter 5 to create a structure for trees:

```
structure IntTree = MkTree (IntItem)
```

We can then instantiate the applications structure:

```
structure IntApps = MkApplications (structure T = IntTree)
```

and also the structure for heaps:

```
structure IntHeap = MkHeap (structure I = IntItem and T = IntTree and
                                                          A = IntApps)
```

Example

As an example of how some of these functions operate, consider forming a complete tree from the following list of integers: [54,25,43,60,16,68]. The evaluation of a call to mkcomplete with these numbers proceeds as shown below, using the flattened infix representation for trees which was introduced in Chapter 5, and where square brackets denote lists, and round brackets, (), denote an empty tree:

```
mkcomplete [54,25,43,60,16,68] ( ) →  mkcomplete [25,43,60,16,68]
                                                    (insert 54 ( ))
```

Now,

```
insert 54 ( ) ≡ cons 54 empty empty
          → (54)
```

∴ mkcomplete [25,43,60,16,68] (insert 54 ( )) → mkcomplete
                                                [25,43,60,16,68] (54)

Now,

```
mkcomplete [25,43,60,16,68] (54) →  mkcomplete [43,60,16,68] (insert
                                                          25 (54))
```

and,

```
insert  25 (54)     → cons  54 (insert  25 ( )) ( )
                    → ((25), 54, ( ))
```

```
∴ mkcomplete [43,60,16,68] (insert 25 (54)) →  mkcomplete [43,60,16,
                                                          68]  ((25),54,( ))
```

and so on:

```
mkcomplete  [43,60,16,68] (54, (25), ( ))
            →   mkcomplete [60,16,68] (insert 43 ((25),54,( )))
            →   mkcomplete [60,16,68] ((25),54,(43))
            →   mkcomplete [16,68] (insert 60 ((25),54,(43)))
            →   mkcomplete [16,68] (((60), 25, ()), 54, (43))
            →   mkcomplete [68] (insert 16 (((60), 25, ()),54,(43)))
            →   mkcomplete [68]  (((60), 25, (16)),54,(43))
            →   mkcomplete [ ] (insert 68 (((60),25,(16)),54,(43)))
            →   mkcomplete [ ]  (((60),25,(16)),54,((68), 43, ()))
            →   (((60),25,(16)),54,((68), 43, ()))
```

The result of this reduction is the tree `(((60),25,(16)),54,((68), 43, ()))`, which
is shown in Figure 6.10.

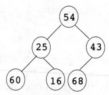

Figure 6.10

To create a heap from this tree, we can use the function `buildheap` which we discussed earlier. The reduction of the call to `buildheap` is shown below:

```
buildheap  (((60),25,(16)),54,((68), 43, ()))
                            → mkheap 54 (buildheap ((60),25,
                              (16))) (buildheap ((68), 43, ()))
```

Considering the left subtree of this expression, we have:

```
buildheap ((60),25,(16)) → mkheap 25 (buildheap (60)) (buildheap
                                                            (16))
```

and

```
buildheap (60)     → mkheap 60 ( ) ( )
                   → (60)
```

and

```
buildheap (16)     → (16)
∴ mkheap 25 (buildheap (60)) (buildheap (16))  → mkheap 25 (60) (16)
                                               → cons 60 (mkheap 25
                                                    ( ) ( )) (16)
```

$$\rightarrow \text{ cons 60 (25) (16)}$$
$$\rightarrow \text{ ((25), 60, (16))}$$

This heap (shown in Figure 6.11) will form the left subtree of the heap under construction.

Figure 6.11

Turning to the right subtree, we have:

```
buildheap ((68), 43, ( ))  → mkheap 43 (buildheap (68)) ()
                           → mkheap 43 (68) ()
                           → cons 68 (43) ()
                           → ((43), 68, ())
```

This second heap is shown in Figure 6.12.

Figure 6.12

Substituting these trees into the initial expression, we have:

```
mkheap 54 (buildheap ((60),25,(16))) (buildheap ((68), 43, ())) →
                   mkheap 54  ((25), 60, (16)) ((43), 68, ())
```

Now,

```
mkheap 54  ((25), 60, (16)) ((43), 68, ( ))  → cons 68 ((25), 60,
                                        (16))  (mkheap 54 (43) ())
                                     → cons 68 ((25), 60,
                                            (16)) (54, (43), ())
                                     → (((25), 60, (16)), 68,
                                             ((43), 54, ()))
```

Thus, the final heap is the tree (((25), 60, (16)), 68, ((43), 54, ())), which is
shown in Figure 6.13.

We will now consider two applications of heaps, the first of which is a sorting
algorithm.

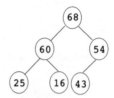

Figure 6.13

Heapsort

An efficient sorting algorithm can be implemented by using a heap. This algorithm, which is called *heapsort* (Williams 1964) has two stages:

1. Convert the data to be sorted into a heap.
2. Successively output the root and restructure the remaining tree into a heap.

For example, suppose we wish to sort the following list of numbers:

    [54,25,43,60,16,68]

As shown in the previous section, we can use the functions developed for manipulating heaps to insert these numbers into a complete tree and then restructure the resulting tree into a heap, resulting in the heap shown in Figure 6.13.

To produce a sorted list, we output the root of the tree, leaving us with two trees which are both heaps. (For example, after removing the root from the heap in Figure 6.13, we are left with the two heaps shown in Figure 6.14.) To reform the heap, we take an item from one of the heaps and use this item and the two heaps (one of which has just had an item removed) as the parameters for the function mkheap. The item which is easiest to remove is the one which is contained in the last node of the tree, i.e. the rightmost node on the lowest level. The advantage of using this node as the new root of the heap is that it will leave a tree which is still complete.

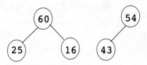

Figure 6.14

The last node of the tree in Figure 6.13 contains the value 43, so this is the value that we use to reform the heap by calling mkheap. The evaluation of the call is shown below:

    mkheap 43 ((25),60,(16))(54)   → cons 60 (mkheap 43 (25)(16)) (54)
                                    → cons 60 (cons 43 (25) (16)) (54)
                                    → (((25), 43, (16)), 60, (54))

which is the heap shown in Figure 6.15.

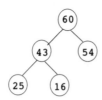

Figure 6.15

In the following section we give a specification for the function heapsort.

Specification

We start by specifying the top level function:

```
val heapsort : tree -> item list
(*Pre: takes a tree which is a heap
   Post: returns an ordered list containing the items in the heap *)
```

Using case analysis, if the tree is empty then there is nothing to do:

```
heapsort empty  = empty
```

If the left and right subtrees are empty, then the tree will be of the form cons i empty empty, where i is the item at the root of the tree. In this case we return the root:

```
heapsort (cons i empty empty) = [i]
```

Otherwise, we must add the root of the tree to the output list and sort the heap which is produced by replacing the root by the last item in the tree, remembering to remove the item (called last in the specification below) from whichever subtree contained it:

```
heapsort (cons i l r) = [i]::heapsort (mkheap last (take last l)
                                              (take
                                               last r))
```

We will need a function which finds the last item in the tree. We will assume that the tree is not empty. The function's heading is given below:

```
val findlast : tree -> item
(*Pre: takes a complete tree which is non-empty
   Post: returns the rightmost item in the lowest level of the tree *)
```

If the subtrees are empty, then the item is at the root of the tree:

```
findlast (cons i empty empty) = i
```

If the heights of the two subtrees are the same, then the last item will be the one furthest to the right (because of the way in which a complete tree is constructed). Otherwise, the last item is contained in the left subtree. This analysis gives us the second case:

```
findlast (cons i l r) = if height l = height r then findlast r
                        else
                        findlast l
```

The only remaining function to specify is the one which returns the tree without the last item, or the unaltered tree if the item is not in the tree.

```
val take : item -> tree -> tree
(*Pre: takes an item (which is the last in the tree) and a complete
   tree
   Post: returns the tree without the item, or the unchanged tree if
   the item is not in the tree *)
```

Again, we will specify this by case analysis, using the fact that the item will be in the right subtree if the subtrees have the same height, and in the left otherwise:

```
take i empty = empty
take i (cons i empty empty) = empty
take i (cons i l r) = if height l = height r then
                        cons i l (take i r)
                      else
                        cons i (take i l) r
```

The implementation of the functions specified above is given in the following section.

Implementation

The implementation of these functions can be included in the functor which we constructed for heap manipulation, and their signatures, together with the pre- and postconditions (which were given as part of their specification), also need to be added to the corresponding signature.

```
fun heapsort t = if isempty t then []
                 else
                 if isempty (left t) andalso isempty (right t) then
                   [root t]
                 else
                 let val r = findlast t
                 in (root t)::heapsort (mkheap r (take r (left t))
                                                 (take r (right t)))
                 end

fun findlast t = if isempty (left t) andalso isempty (right t) then
                   (root t)
                 else
                 if height (left t) = height (right t) then
                   findlast (right t)
                 else
                 findlast (left t)

fun take i t = if isempty t orelse I.isequal i (root t) then empty
               else
               if height (left t) = height (right t) then
                 cons (root t) (left t) (take i (right t))
```

```
          else
            cons (root t) (take i (left t)) (right t)
```

Efficiency

A complete binary tree with n nodes has a height of $O(\log_2 n)$. To create the initial heap we have to call mkheap for every node. So the maximum number of comparisons and swaps for this stage is $O(n \log_2 n)$. Each time a value is removed from the heap there will be $O(\log_2 n)$ comparisons, and this happens n times. So overall the efficiency of heapsort is $O(n \log_2 n)$, as constants are not significant in asymptotic analyses.

This is the worst case analysis; heapsort compares well with algorithms such as quicksort, which has $O(n \log_2 n)$ performance on average, but $O(n^2)$ performance in the worst case.

Priority Queues

We can use a heap to implement the priority queue ADT, where the ordering on the items is that of their priorities. For example, consider the heap in Figure 6.16 (in which only the items' priorities are shown).

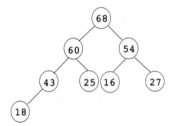

Figure 6.16

Removing an item from the front of the priority queue means removing the item with highest priority, i.e. the one at the root of the tree. This will leave two disjoint heaps which will then have to be transformed back into a single heap. As we discussed for the heapsort algorithm, the node which is easiest to remove is the last node of the tree (the node which contains the value 18 in Figure 6.16). We can then use the function mkheap which takes an item and two heaps and returns a heap.

Turning to the efficiency of this algorithm, in the worst case the number of comparisons we will have to do is equal to the height of the tree. As was shown in the last chapter, the height of a complete binary tree is less than or equal to $\log_2(n + 1)$, where n is the number of nodes in the tree.

The fact that a heap is always balanced means that it is a very efficient implementation of a priority queue, although deletion would still be faster with the ordered tree implementation which we discussed earlier, provided that the tree remains balanced.

EXERCISES 6.3

1. Reduce the following expression to normal form, showing all working:

```
buildheap (mkcomplete [12,8,4,6,7,21,3] empty)
```

2. Change the implementation of heapsort so that it uses an auxiliary function called sort, which takes an accumulating parameter:

```
val sort : tree ->  item list  -> item list
(*Pre: takes a tree and a list which is empty initially
   Post: returns a sorted list of items *)
```

BALANCED SEARCH TREES

The efficiency of the operations which we have discussed for searching and sorting depends crucially on the height of the tree. Consequently it is extremely important to try to ensure that the tree remains balanced. A complete binary tree is balanced, but we would like to relax the restriction that states that the nodes must be filled from left to right on the lowest level. The kind of balanced search tree which we are going to discuss in the next section enables us to do this, and remains balanced in *all* situations, so that it can always be searched efficiently.

AVL Trees: Height Balanced Trees

AVL trees, or *height balanced trees,* are named after Adelson-Velskii and Landis (1962), who gave the definition of height balance for ordered trees which is given below. They also described algorithms for inserting and deleting nodes without disturbing the balance of the tree. In nearly all cases the average path length of an AVL tree approximates to that of a complete ordered tree.

Because the tree is height balanced, operations to retrieve, insert and delete an item are all proportional to $O(\log_2 n)$ time, where n is the number of nodes. The tree remains height balanced after the operations.

Definitions

A tree is *height balanced* or *AVL* if it is empty or if both its left and right subtrees are height balanced and the difference in the heights of its left and right subtrees is less than or equal to one, i.e.

| height (left subtree) − height (right subtree) | ≤ 1

Horowitz and Sahni (1976) defined the *balance factor* of a node in a binary tree to be:

height (left subtree) − height (right subtree)

So, for an AVL tree, the balance factor of a node is either 1, 0, or -1. AVL trees can be used to implement trees in which the items are ordered so that the values in the left sub-tree of a node are less than the value at that node, and those in the right subtree are greater. Figure 6.17 shows two such trees; note that the trees shown are, in fact, both ordered binary trees.

We can reuse the algebraic specification of the ordered binary tree, given earlier in the chapter, in the specification and implementation of such AVL trees. The operation of inserting an item into an ordered AVL tree in such a way that the resulting tree is still height balanced is not trivial, and is considered in the next subsection.

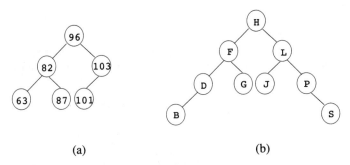

(a)   (b)

Figure 6.17 Two AVL trees

Inserting an item

Inserting an item into a tree may result in a tree which is still balanced, or it may cause the balance factor of a subtree to become 2 or −2, which means that rebalancing is required. The rebalancing must be such that:

1. The inorder traversal of the new tree is the same as that of the original tree.
2. The transformed tree must be height balanced.

The rebalancing is done by means of a number of rotations, of which there are two sorts, *right* and *left*. In a *right* rotation, the root of the tree moves down and to the right, its position being taken by the root of the left subtree, the right subtree of which becomes the previous root's left subtree (see Figure 6.18).

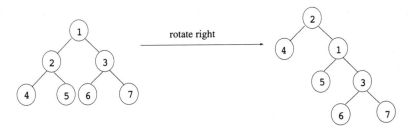

Figure 6.18

Note that the inorder traversal of the tree on the left, (4 2 5 1 6 3 7), is the same as that of the tree on the right.

The specification of the `rotate_right` algorithm is given below:

```
val rotate_right : tree -> tree

rotate_right empty  = empty
rotate_right (cons i l r) = cons (root l) (left  l) (cons i
                                                    (right l ) r )
```

In a *left* rotation, on the other hand, the root of the tree moves down and to the left, its position being taken by the root of its right subtree, the right subtree of which becomes the (old) root's right subtree (see Figure 6.19).

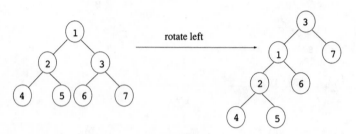

Figure 6.19

The specification of this `rotate_left` algorithm is the mirror image of the one given for right rotation:

```
val rotate_left : tree -> tree

rotate_left  empty = empty
rotate_left (cons i l r) = cons (root r ) (cons i l (left r))
                                                    (right r )
```

Again the inorder traversal of the two trees is the same.

It may be necessary to use several rotations in order to rebalance the tree.

Example

Figure 6.20 shows an ordered tree into which an item with a priority of 15 has just been inserted, using the `insert` function specified for ordered trees at the beginning of this chapter.

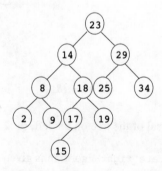

Figure 6.20

The balance factor of the root of the tree is now 2 and so the tree is no longer height balanced.

To transform the tree back in to an AVL tree we must use two rotations, starting with a left rotation about the node containing the value 14 to produce the tree in Figure 6.21 (in which the figures above two of the nodes indicate their balance factors). This is followed by a right rotation about the node containing the value 23 to produce the AVL tree in Figure 6.22.

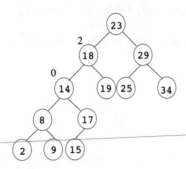

Figure 6.21 Left rotation about 14

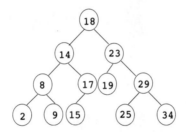

Figure 6.22 Right rotation about 23

Note that the inorder traversal of this tree (2 8 9 14 15 17 18 19 23 25 29 34) is the same as that of the tree with which we started.

SUMMARY

- An *ordered tree* is a binary tree which has an ordering imposed on the nodes such that, for each node:
  - All values in its left subtree are less than the value in that node, and
  - all values in its right subtree are greater than the value in that node.
- Ordered binary trees can be used to write efficient sorting and searching routines, and to implement other ADTs, such as priority queues.
- A *heap* is a complete binary tree which has an ordering imposed on its nodes such that the value at the root of the tree is greater than or equal to the values of both of its children, and both subtrees are heaps, together with a number of access functions.

- An efficient sorting algorithm can be implemented by using a heap. The algorithm called *heapsort* has two stages:
  - Convert the data to be sorted into a heap.
  - Successively output the root and restructure the remaining tree into a heap.
- A heap can be used to implement a priority queue.
- A tree is *height balanced* if it is empty or if both its left and right subtrees are height balanced and the difference in the heights of its left and right subtrees is less than or equal to one.
- Height balanced trees are also called *AVL* trees, after Adelson-Velskii and Landis.

CHAPTER 7

2-3 Trees

INTRODUCTION

The definition of the ADT binary tree given in Chapter 5 stated that each node has at most two subtrees. In this chapter we discuss a more general ADT in which the number of items in a node may vary between one and two, and the number of subtrees of a node can vary between two and three, giving the ADT the name *2-3 tree*.

We have already seen how the efficiency with which an ordered tree can be used to store and retrieve sorted data depends on whether the tree is balanced. A 2-3 tree is similar to an AVL tree in that it remains balanced in all situations; whenever the tree becomes unbalanced because of an insertion or a deletion it is immediately rebalanced so that the heights of all the subtrees are the same. However, because a node in a 2-3 tree can contain either one or two items, it is easier to maintain the shape of such a tree on insertion of an item than it is to maintain that of the trees discussed so far. A 2-3 tree will only grow (that is, its height will increase) if all the nodes in the tree contain two items. We will examine the insertion algorithm later in detail.

We start with a more formal definition of a 2-3 tree.

DEFINITION

The ADT *2-3 tree* is a finite set of nodes which is either empty, or consists of a root containing one item and two disjoint subtrees, or consists of a root containing two items and three disjoint subtrees, where the subtrees are 2-3 trees of the same height, together with a number of access functions.

REPRESENTATION AND NOTATION

We will use the same notation for 2-3 trees as we did for binary trees except that we will refer to the subtrees as *left*, *middle* and *right*.

For example, Figure 7.1 shows a 2-3 tree in which the values in the nodes have an ordering imposed on them (which is similar to that imposed on the values in an ordered binary tree). All the values in the left subtree of a node are less than the value (or values) at the node, all values in the right subtree are greater than the value (or values) at the node, and all those in a middle subtree (where one exists) are such that they lie between the two values in the node. In fact this tree is an example of a *2-3 search tree*, which is an extension of an ordered binary tree, and which will be defined more formally later.

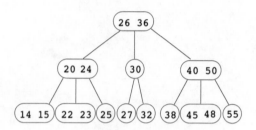

Figure 7.1 A 2-3 tree

Note that if a node has two subtrees then it must contain only one item, whereas if it has three subtrees then it must contain two items.

From the fact that the subtrees have the same height, it follows that a 2-3 tree of height h always has at least as many nodes as a full binary tree of height h; that is, it always has at least $(2^h - 1)$ nodes.

ALGEBRAIC SPECIFICATION

We can use the specification of the binary tree ADT as the foundation for the specification of the 2-3 tree. We will need additional functions to deal with the middle subtree and the fact that the root may contain either one or two items. The entire specification which we will use is given below.

Syntax of the Access Functions

Four of the access functions are identical to four of those given for the ADT binary tree:

```
val empty : tree
(*Post: returns an empty tree *)

val isempty : tree -> bool
(*Post: returns true if t is empty,otherwise false *)

val left : tree -> tree
(*Post: returns the left subtree *)

val right : tree -> tree
(*Post: returns the right subtree  *)
```

In addition to these we will need another selector function:

```
val middle : tree -> tree
(*Post: returns the middle subtree  *)
```

The selector function root must now be restricted to trees which have only one item at their root:

```
val root : tree -> item
(*Pre: takes a tree which has one item at its root
  Post: returns the data item at the root   *)
```

Consequently we will need new selector functions to deal with trees which have two items at their root:

```
val first : tree -> item
(*Pre: takes a tree which has two items at its root
  Post: returns the first item in the root   *)

val second : tree -> item
(*Pre: takes a tree which has two items at its root
  Post: returns the second item in the root  *)
```

Similarly, cons is restricted to constructing trees which have only one item at their root:

```
val cons : item -> tree -> tree -> tree
(*Pre: takes an item and two trees
  Post: returns a tree which has the item  at its root and l and r as
  its left and right subtrees, where l and r are the 1st and 2nd
  parameters of type tree respectively*)
```

and we need a new constructor function to construct trees with two items at the root:

```
val cons2 : item -> item -> tree -> tree -> tree -> tree
(*Pre: takes two items and three trees
  Post: returns a tree which has the items at its root and l, m, r as
  its left, middle and right subtrees, where l, m and r are the 1st,
  2nd and 3rd parameters of type tree respectively *)
```

Finally, we will need a determinant function which we can use to determine the number of items at the root of a tree:

```
val numvals : tree -> int
(*Post: returns either 1 or 2, i.e. the number of items at the root of
  the tree *)
```

Semantics of the Access Functions

The axioms describing the semantics of the access functions are very similar to those for the binary tree, the only difference being that a 2-3 tree has three constructors and so can have one of three forms: empty, (cons i l r) or (cons2 i j l m r) where i and j are items, l, m, and r are trees. The action of the access functions for each of these cases is specified below.

```
1.   isempty empty  = true
2.   isempty (cons i l r) = false
```

```
3.    isempty (cons2 i j l m r) = false
4.    root empty = error
5.    root (cons i l r) = i
6.    root (cons2 i j l m r) = error
7.    first empty = error
8.    first (cons i l r) = error
9.    first (cons2 i j l m r) = i
10.   second empty = error
11.   second (cons i l r) = error
12.   second (cons2 i j l m r) = j
13.   left empty = error
14.   left  (cons i l r) = l
15.   left (cons2 i j l m r) = l
16.   right empty = error
17.   right (cons i l r)  = r
18.   right (cons2 i j l m r) = r
19.   middle empty  = error
20.   middle (cons i l r) = error
21.   middle (cons2 i j l m r) = m
22.   numvals empty = error
23.   numvals  (cons i l r) = 1
24.   numvals  (cons2 i j l m r) = 2
```

APPLICATIONS

There are several reasons for our interest in 2-3 trees. One is that they are an example of a
data type which can be used to implement a table stored in external memory (such as a
disk). This data type is called a *B-tree* (Bayer and McCreight, 1972), and its structure is
such that it can have any number of items in each node. If the number of items held in
each node is at most two then each node has a maximum of three subtrees, in which case
the B-tree (which is said to be of *order* three) is identical to a 2-3 tree. Figure 7.2 illustrates how the access functions can be used to construct application functions.

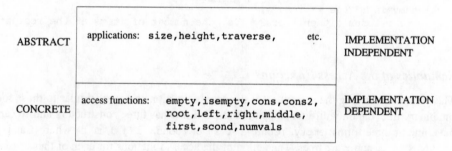

Figure 7.2

Since 2-3 search trees remain perfectly balanced at all times, they can be searched very
efficiently ($O(\log_2 n)$, where n is the number of items in the tree). Consequently they can
be used as an efficient implementation of a number of other ADTs.

IMPLEMENTATION

We will assume that the items in the tree have the following signature:

```
signature ITEM =
  sig
  eqtype item
  val isequal : item -> item -> bool
  (*Post: returns true if the items are equal *)
  val isless : item -> item -> bool
  (*Post: returns true if the 1st item is smaller than the 2nd *)
  val isgreater : item -> item -> bool
  (*Post: returns true if the 1st item is larger than the 2nd *)
  val showitem : item -> string
  (*Post: a display function which returns a string *)
  val format : string -> string list -> unit
  (*Post: opens a file and outputs a list of strings to it *)
  end
```

The constraint signature for the ADT 2-3 tree will be of the following form:

```
signature TREE =
  sig
  structure I : ITEM
  open I (*opens the structure I for use *)
  type tree
  val empty : tree
  (*Post: returns an empty tree *)
  val isempty : tree -> bool
  (*Post: returns true if t is empty,otherwise false *)
  val cons : item -> tree -> tree -> tree
  (*Pre: takes an item and two trees
    Post: returns a tree which has the item  at its root and l and r
    as its left and right subtrees, where l and r are the 1st and 2nd
    parameters  of type tree respectively*)
  val cons2 : item -> item -> tree -> tree -> tree -> tree
  (*Pre: takes two items and three trees
    Post: returns a tree which has the items at its root and l, m, r
    as its left, middle and right subtrees, where l, m and r are the
    1st, 2nd and 3rd parameters  of type tree respectively *)
  val left : tree -> tree
  (*Post: returns the left subtree *)
  val right : tree -> tree
  (*Post: returns the right subtree  *)
  val middle : tree -> tree
  (*Post: returns the middle subtree  *)
  val root : tree -> item
  (*Pre: takes a tree which has one item at its root
    Post: returns the data item at the root    *)
  val first : tree -> item
  (*Pre: takes a tree which has two items at its root
    Post: returns the first item in the root    *)
  val second : tree -> item
  (*Pre: takes a tree which has two items at its root
    Post: returns the second item in the root   *)
  val numvals : tree -> int
  (*Post: returns either 1 or 2, i.e. the number of items at the root
    of the tree *)
```

```
    val showtree : tree -> string list
    (*Post: formats a tree for output to a text stream *)
    val show : tree -> string
    (*Post: formats a tree for output to the standard output stream *)
end
```

We will encapsulate the access functions within a functor called MkTree. The abstype declaration for the ADT will reflect the definition given at the start of the chapter, in that the data type has three data constructors, called Empty, Tree and TwoThree. The functor is parameterised over the type ITEM. Thus we have the following functor heading and abstype declaration:

```
functor MkTree (Itemstruct : ITEM) : TREE =
struct
structure I = Itemstruct     (*indicates that this item structure is the
                               same as that used in the signature*)

abstype tree = Empty
             | Tree of tree * I.item * tree
             | TwoThree of I.item * I.item * tree * tree * tree
```

The access functions can be implemented by case analysis, using the algebraic specification. There are now three cases to consider for each function, as the tree can have three possible forms. The constructor functions and predicate functions are straightforward to implement:

```
val empty = Empty

fun cons i l r = Tree (l,i,r)

fun cons2 i j l m r = TwoThree (i,j,l,m,r)

fun  isempty Empty = true
   | isempty (Tree t) = false
   | isempty (TwoThree t) = false
```

The selector functions left, middle and right all have to return the appropriate sub-tree. For example:

```
fun left (Tree (l,i,r)) = l
   | left (TwoThree (i,j,l,m,r)) = l
   | left Empty = hd []
```

whereas the functions root, first and second have to return the appropriate data items. For example:

```
fun root (Tree (l,i,r)) = i
   | root (TwoThree (i,j,l,m,r)) = hd []
   | root Empty = hd []

fun first (Tree (l,i,r)) = hd []
   | first (TwoThree (i,j,l,m,r)) = i
   | first Empty = hd []
```

and similarly for the function second.

The function numvals returns the number of values in the root:

```
fun numvals (Tree (l,i,r)) = 1
  | numvals (TwoThree (i,j,l,m,r)) = 2
  | numvals Empty = 0
```

The display functions are a straightforward extension of those given for binary trees in Chapter 5, and so will not be repeated here.

Verification and Validation

We can verify the implementation of the access functions during their development by comparing the implementation with the algebraic specification, and by rewriting calls to the functions with arbitrary instances of 2-3 trees.

To validate the implementation, we could provide a simple integer structure for the items in the 2-3 tree (such as the IntItem structure given in Chapter 5), and pass this as a parameter to the MkTree functor:

```
structure IntTree = MkTree (IntItem)
```

and then use this structure to test the implementation of the access functions, again using the algebraic specification as an oracle.

Applying the Generic ADT

As a simple example of the application of the access functions, consider the development of a function to return the height of a 2-3 tree:

```
val height  : tree -> int
(*Pre: takes a 2-3 tree
  Post: returns the height of the tree *)
```

We can specify the function by case analysis:

```
height empty = 0
height (cons i l r) = 1 + max2 (height l) (height r)
height (cons2 i j l m r) = 1 + max3 (height l)   (height m) (height r)
```

where max2 and max3 are functions (supplied as part of our library) which return the largest of two or three integers, respectively.

We will implement this function within a functor called MkApplications which is constrained by a signature which acts as its interface, such as the one shown below:

```
signature APPS =
  sig
  structure T : TREE
  open T
  val height : tree -> int
  (*Pre: takes a 2-3 tree
    Post: returns the height of the tree *)
  end
```

The functor itself will be parameterised over a structure with signature TREE, as it will need to use the 2-3 tree access functions. The functor is shown below:

```
functor MkApplications (structure T: TREE) : APPS =
struct
structure T = T
open T

fun height t =  if isempty t then 0
                else
                if numvals t = 1 then
                    1 + max2 (height(left t)) (height(right t))
                else
                    1 + max3 (height(left t)) (height(middle t)) (height
                                                              (right t))

end
```

The line:

```
structure T = T
```

informs the compiler that the structure T is the same as the one which the signature APPS uses.

We can then instantiate this applications functor in the same way as usual. For example, for a 2-3 tree of integers, we need to create a structure by using the IntTree structure:

```
structure IntApps = MkApplications (structure T = IntTree)
```

and we can use this structure to evaluate (for example) the height of the 2-3 tree in Figure 7.3, with an expression of the form:

```
height (cons2 20 30 (cons2 7 13 (cons2 1 3 empty empty empty)
        (cons2 8 10 empty empty empty) (cons2 14 16 empty empty empty))
        (cons 25 (cons 21 empty empty) (cons 27 empty empty))
        (cons 42 (cons 35 empty empty) (cons 45 empty empty)))
```

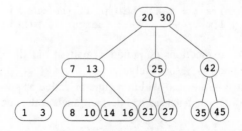

Figure 7.3

EXERCISE 7.1

1. Complete the implementation of the access functions for the 2-3 tree ADT, and validate the implementation using the algebraic specification.

We will now go on to discuss the ADT *2-3 search tree*, which was mentioned briefly at the start of the chapter.

2-3 SEARCH TREES

Definition

The ADT *2-3 search tree* is a 2-3 tree which has an ordering imposed on the values in the nodes such that, if there is one item at the root, all values in its left subtree are less than the value at the root, and all values in its right subtree are greater than the value at the root, and both subtrees are also 2-3 search trees. Otherwise, if there are two items at the root of the tree, the smaller value of the two must be greater than all values in the left subtree and less than all values in the middle subtree, and the larger of the two must be greater than all values in the middle subtree and less than all values in the right subtree. Again all the subtrees must be 2-3 search trees.

Thus a 2-3 search tree is an extended form of the ordered binary tree.

Algebraic Specification

The algebraic specification of the 2-3 search tree can be constructed by reusing that of the 2-3 tree. The necessary additional access functions are specified below.

Syntax

We will need two new selector functions which enable us to select the smallest and largest values in a node which contains two values:

```
val minval : tree -> item
(*Pre: takes a 2-3 tree which has a node containing 2 values at its
  root
  Post: returns the smallest of the two values *)

val maxval : tree -> item
(*Pre: takes a 2-3 tree which has a node containing 2 values at its
  root
  Post: returns the largest of the two values *)
```

A constructor function is required which will ensure that when an item is inserted into a 2-3 search tree the values in the tree remain ordered and the tree remains balanced. The function heading is given below:

```
val insert : item -> tree -> tree
(*Pre: takes an item and a 2-3 search tree.
  Post: returns a 2-3 search tree with the item inserted in the
  correct position *)
```

A function to construct a 2-3 search tree from a list of items may also be needed:

```
val build : item list -> tree -> tree
(*Pre: takes a list of items and a tree which is initially empty.
  Post: returns a 2-3 search tree with the items inserted in the
  correct positions *)
```

Semantics

In the following, i, j and k denote items and l, m and r denote 2-3 trees.

We can specify the function minval as follows:

```
minval empty = error
minval (cons i l r) = error
minval (cons2 i j l m r) = min i j
```

where min is a function which returns the smallest of two items. As this is a type-dependent function it must be provided within the structures which are used to instantiate the signature ITEM.

Similarly, the specification of the function maxval requires a function max which returns the largest of two items.

```
maxval empty = error
maxval (cons i l r) = error
maxval (cons2 i j l m r) = max i j
```

We will specify the insert function by using case analysis and the access functions for 2-3 trees. The easiest case to specify occurs when the tree is empty. We can specify this as:

```
insert  i empty = cons  i empty empty
```

If the tree has only one value at the root and the subtrees are empty then we can simply insert the new item into the root of the tree and return a 2-3 tree with the two items at the root:

```
insert i (cons j empty empty) = cons2 i j empty empty empty
```

If the tree consists of only two values, then we return a binary tree with one value in each node. We will assume the existence of the comparison functions min and max which return the smallest and largest values of two items respectively, and mid, which takes three items, compares their size and returns the value in the middle.

```
insert i (cons2  j k empty empty empty) = cons (mid i j k)
                                     (cons (min (min j k) i)
                                                  empty empty)
                                     (cons (max (max  j k) i)
                                                  empty empty)
```

Now we must consider the cases which may arise if the subtrees are not empty. Finding the correct position to insert the item is simple: we just compare the item with the value or values at the root and call insert recursively in the way which we did with the ordered tree insertion function. However, we must also ensure that the resulting tree is a 2-3 tree. This may mean reshaping the tree to ensure that all the subtrees of the root are of the same height. We will assume that we have a function called reform which can be used to rebalance the tree if necessary:

```
val reform : tree -> tree
(*Post: returns a 2-3 search tree *)
```

Continuing with the specification of the `insert` function, we now suppose that there is only one value at the root and that the subtrees are not empty:

```
insert  i (cons j l r) = if i < j then
                               reform (cons j (insert i l ) r)
                         else
                         reform (cons  j  l  (insert i r))
```

The case of insertion into a tree with two values at the root is simply an extension of this:

```
insert  i (cons2 j k l m r) = if i < (min j k)  then
                                   reform (cons2 j k (insert  i l)
                                                               m r )
                              else
                              if i > (min j k) and i < (max j k)  then
                                   reform (cons2 j k l (insert i m) r )
                              else
                              reform (cons2  j k l m  (insert  i r ))
```

Note that the search for the correct place to insert an item always ends at a leaf, and a tree only grows in height if we are inserting an item into a node which already contains two items. When this happens, the new subtree contains one value at its root and has two subtrees. Since the tree is reshaped after each insertion it will never grow by more than one level before it is rebalanced.

The function `build` can be specified by case analysis over a list using the function `insert`:

```
build [] t = t
build (x::xs) t = build xs (insert x t)
```

We now turn our attention to the `reform` function. The function for insertion is typical of many tree manipulation algorithms, in that the tree is traversed until a leaf is found. (This common algorithmic design is enforced by the access functions provided for the ADT tree.) In designing the function `reform` we will follow this pattern, traversing the tree until a subtree which can be rebalanced is found. However, this is not the end of the story, because the result of rebalancing the subtree may be a tree which is still unbalanced, necessitating another rebalancing. The only trees which can be rebalanced without such recursive calls are those of height less than or equal to three. Consequently we will specify a function (called `reshape`) to cope with this case first.

```
val reshape: tree -> tree
(*Pre: reshapes a tree of ht <=3, which has grown due to an
  insertion *)
(*Post: returns a 2-3 search tree *)
```

There is no need to reshape an empty tree:

```
reshape empty = empty
```

Suppose that there is only one item in the node at the root of the tree. If the height of the two subtrees is the same then again there is no need to reshape the tree:

```
reshape (cons i l r) = if height  l = height  r  then
                            (cons i l r)
```

Otherwise if the height of the left subtree is greater than the height of the right, then we must find a way of rebalancing the left subtree. As there is only one value at the root, we can do this by taking the root of the left subtree and inserting it into the root of the tree, creating a 2-3 tree with two values at the root. We use the subtrees of the left subtree to form the left and middle subtrees of the new tree. The right subtree is the same as it was in the original tree. So the specification is:

```
if height  l > height  r  then
    cons2 (root l) i (left l) (right l) r
```

This has the effect of reducing the height of the left subtree while maintaining the ordering imposed on the nodes. All the values in the new left subtree will be less then the smallest value in the root, because that value was the root of the left subtree. Similarly, all values in the middle subtree are greater than the smallest value in the root and less than the largest value. The right subtree remains unchanged and so all the items in the right subtree are greater than both values in the root of the tree. Note that the tree has not grown in height.

If the height of the right subtree is greater than the height of the left then the algorithm for rebalancing is the mirror image of the one above. The specification of the entire algorithm for a root which only contains one item is given below:

```
reshape (cons i l r) =  if height  l = height  r  then
                            (cons i l r)
                        else if height  l > height  r  then
                            cons2 (root l) i (left l) (right l) r
                        else
                            cons2  i (root r)  l  (left r)  (right r)
```

Now suppose that the root contains two items and has three subtrees. The method for reshaping the tree is an extension of the cases explained above. If the heights of the three subtrees are all the same then the tree does not need reshaping:

```
reshape (cons2 i j l m r)  = if height l  = height m  = height r  then
                                (cons2 i j l m r)
```

If the left subtree has grown due to the insertion of an item, then we rebalance the tree by forming a tree with only one value at the root and only two subtrees. Because the unbalancing occurred due to the growth of the left subtree, we choose the smallest value in the root to form the new root. The left subtree stays as it is. The right subtree is formed from the larger of the two items in the root, and the middle and right subtrees of the original tree. The specification is given below:

```
if height l  > height m and height l  > height  r  then
    cons  (min i j) l (cons (max i j) m r)
```

The algorithm for reshaping when the middle subtree has increased in height due to an insertion is analogous to the one above. This time, however, the item at the new root of the tree must be the item which was at the root of the middle subtree; this we know to be a single value, because of the operational semantics of `insert`. The left subtree is formed from the smaller of the two values in the root, the left subtree of the tree and the left subtree of what was the middle subtree. The right subtree is formed from the larger of the two values in the root, the right subtree of what was the middle subtree, and the right subtree of the original tree:

```
if height  m  > height  r and height  m  > height  l  then
     cons (root  m ) (cons (min i j)  l  (left m)) (cons (max i j)
                                                    (right m)  r)
```

The final case to consider occurs when the right subtree has grown. In this case we take the larger of the two values at the root to be the new root, and construct the left subtree from the smaller of the two values and the left and middle subtrees of the original tree. The right subtree stays exactly as it is:

```
else
cons (max i j) (cons  (min i j) l m) r
```

Thus the complete specification for the `reshape` algorithm is:

```
reshape empty = empty
reshape (cons i l r) =  if height  l  = height  r  then
                          (cons i l r)
                        else if height  l  > height  r  then
                          cons2 (root l ) i (left l ) (right l) r
                        else
                          cons2  i (root r)  l  (left r)  (right r)
reshape (cons2 i j l m r)  = if height l  = height m  = height r then
                          (cons2 i j l m r)
                        else
                        if height l  > height m and height l  >
                                                   height  r  then
                          cons  (min i j) l (cons (max i j)
                                                        m r)
                        else
                        if height  m  > height  r and height  m
                                              > height  l  then
                          cons (root  m )
                          (cons (min i j)  l  (left m))
                          (cons (max i j)  (right m) r)
                        else
                        cons (max i j) (cons  (min i j) l m) r
```

As we mentioned previously, the function `reshape` is only appropriate for trees of height less than or equal to three. Consequently it must be called by another function, which takes the height of the tree into consideration. The function's heading is given below:

```
val  rebalance : tree -> int -> tree
(*Pre: takes a tree and an integer which is initially 3 *)
(*Post: returns a 2-3 search tree *)
```

If the height of the tree is less than or equal to the integer parameter (which is initially three), then we can simply call reshape:

```
rebalance n t = if height t <= n then reshape t
```

Otherwise, if there is one value at the root, there are three cases to consider: either the left subtree has greater height than the right, or vice versa, or the tree is balanced. In the first case, we must rebalance the left subtree first, before calling rebalance again, but this time increasing its integer parameter by one. In this way we ensure that the first time the function reshape is called, the height of the tree is three, and the next time, the height is four, and so on, until the tree is finally balanced. Similarly, if the right subtree has grown, we rebalance that one first. This analysis gives us the following specification:

```
rebalance n (cons i l r) = if height l > height r then
                    rebalance (cons i (rebalance l n) r) (n+1)
                  else
                  if height r > height l then
                    rebalance (cons i l (rebalance r n)) (n+1)
                  else
                    cons i l r
```

Similar reasoning leads us to the the following specification for rebalancing when there are two values at the root:

```
rebalance n (cons2 i j l m r) = if height l > height r and  height l >
                                                     height m then
                      rebalance (cons2 i j
                        (rebalance l n) m r) (n+1)
                  else
                  if height m >  height l and
                     height m >  height r then
                      rebalance (cons2 i j
                        l (rebalance m n) r) (n+1)
                  else
                  rebalance (cons2 i j
                        l m (rebalance  r  n)) (n+1)
```

Thus, the entire specification for the function rebalance is:

```
rebalance n t = if height t <= n then reshape t
rebalance n (cons i l r) = if height l > height r then
                    rebalance (cons i (rebalance l n) r)
                                                  (n+1)
                  else
                  if height r > height l then
                    rebalance (cons i l (rebalance r n))
                                                  (n+1)
                  else
                    cons i l r
rebalance n (cons2 i j l m r) = if height l > height r and  height l >
                                                     height m then
```

```
                        rebalance (cons2 i j
                            (rebalance l n) m r) (n+1)
                    else
                    if height m >  height l and
                        height m >  height r then
                        rebalance (cons2 i j
                            l  (rebalance m n) r) (n+1)
                    else
                            rebalance (cons2 i j
                            l m (rebalance  r  n)) (n+1)
```

Finally, we can now specify the function reform, by calling rebalance with the integer
parameter instantiated as three:

```
reform t = rebalance t 3
```

Examples

Suppose that we want to rewrite the following expression (which inserts the value 11 into
the tree in Figure 7.4) to normal form:

```
insert 11 (cons2 7 13 (cons2 1 3 empty empty empty)
(cons2 8 10 empty empty empty) (cons2 14 16 empty empty empty))
```

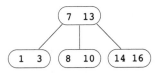

Figure 7.4

Representing the tree using prefix notation, the expression to be rewritten is:

```
insert 11 (7, 13, (1,3), (8,10), (14,16)
```

Now,

```
(insert 11 (7, 13, (1,3), (8,10), (14,16)) →  reform (cons2 7 13
                                              (1,3) (insert 11 (8,10)) (14,16))
```

and

```
(insert 11 (8,10))  →    cons (mid 8 11 10) (cons (min 8 11) empty
                                                                empty)
                         (cons (max 10 11) empty empty)
                    →   (10, (8), (11))
```

∴ `reform (cons2 7 13 (1,3) (insert 11 (8,10)) (14,16))`
      →   `reform (cons2 7 13 (1,3) (10, (8), (11)) (14,16))`
      →   `reform (7, 13,(1,3), (10, (8), (11)), (14,16))`

The tree which is passed to the function `reform` (shown in Figure 7.5) is no longer a 2-3 tree search tree, because the middle subtree has grown in height. However, all of the items are in their correct positions according to their numerical ordering.

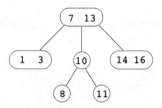

Figure 7.5

The function `reform` calls the function `rebalance`, which (because the height of the tree is three) simply calls the function `reshape`:

`reform (7, 13, (1,3), (10, (8), (11)), (14,16))` → `reshape (7, 13,`
                    `(1,3), (10, (8), (11)), (14,16))`

From the reshape algorithm, we have:

`reshape (7, 13, (1,3), (10, (8), (11)), (14,16))`
         → `cons 10 (cons 7 (1,3)  (8)) (cons 13 (11) (14,16))`
         → `(10, (7, (1,3), (8)), (13, (11), (14,16)))`

This final tree is shown in Figure 7.6.

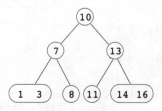

Figure 7.6

Note that a 2-3 search tree only grows in height during insertion if all the nodes on the path from the root to the leaf into which the new item will be inserted contain two items. When it does grow, the tree is reshaped so that all the subtrees of the root have the same height.

Applications

Only the access functions given by the algebraic specification will be made available for general use, to ensure that the ability to reshape 2-3 search trees is restricted to the implementors of the ADT. Figure 7.7 shows the hierarchy of software which can be constructed by using the 2-3 tree access functions.

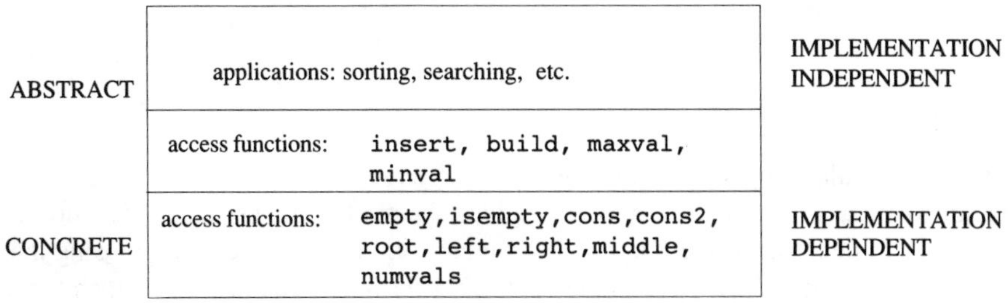

ABSTRACT	applications: sorting, searching, etc.	IMPLEMENTATION INDEPENDENT
	access functions: `insert, build, maxval, minval`	
CONCRETE	access functions: `empty,isempty,cons,cons2, root,left,right,middle, numvals`	IMPLEMENTATION DEPENDENT

Figure 7.7

Let us suppose that the items in the 2-3 search tree are large data structures consisting of a set of information and a unique search key which is an integer, and that we want to write a function to retrieve an item with a particular key from the tree. We will also assume that the item is known to be in the tree.

Retrieving an item from a 2-3 search tree is similar to retrieval from an ordered tree. We first inspect the item at the root of the tree, and if this has the correct key, then we have finished. Otherwise, there are two cases to consider: the root either has one or two items. In the former case we search either the left subtree or the right, depending on whether the item we are looking for is less than or greater than the item at the root. If there are two items in the root, the procedure is very similar, except that we have the possibility that the desired item may be in the middle subtree. We will assume the existence of a function called key which returns the integer key associated with an item:

```
val key : item -> int
(*Post: takes an item and returns its integer key *)
```

The complete specification is given below.

```
val find : int -> tree -> item
(*Pre: takes an integer key and a 2-3 search tree
  Post: returns the information associated with the key *)

find  n (cons i l r)  =  if n = (key i) then i
                         else
                         if n < (key i) then
                             find n l
                         else
                         find n r
find  n  (cons2 i j l m r) = if n = (key i) then i
                             else
```

```
if n = (key j) then j
else
if n < (key i) then
    find   n l
else
if i > min (key i) (key j) and
        n < max (key i) (key j) then
    find n m
else
find n r
```

Implementation

We will encapsulate the access functions for 2-3 search trees within a functor which is constrained by a signature. The signature gives the syntax of the access functions, and thus acts as an interface to the functor. The functor will be constructed by reusing the 2-3 tree access functions which were implemented earlier in the chapter, and which have the signature TREE.

We will use the following signature for the items in the tree:

```
signature ITEM =
  sig
  eqtype item
  val isequal : item -> item -> bool
  (*Post: returns true if the items are equal *)
  val isless : item -> item -> bool
  (*Post: returns true if the 1st item is smaller than the 2nd *)
  val isgreater : item -> item -> bool
  (*Post: returns true if the 1st item is larger than the 2nd *)
  val min : item -> item -> item
  (*Post: takes 2  items and returns the smallest *)
  val max : item -> item -> item
  (*Post: takes 2  items and returns the largest *)
  val mid : item -> item -> item -> item
  (*Post: takes 3  items and returns the middle value *)
  val key : item -> int
  (*Post: takes an item and returns its integer key *)
  val showitem : item -> string
  (*Post: a display function which returns a string *)
  val format : string -> string list -> unit
  (*Post: opens a file and outputs a list of strings to it *)
  end
```

The constraining signature for the functor containing the 2-3 search tree implementation (which is called MkOrd) is as follows:

```
signature ORD =
  sig
  structure I : ITEM
  structure T : TREE
  open I
  open T
  val minval : tree -> item
```

```
(*Pre: takes a 2-3 tree which has a node containing 2 values at its
   root
   Post: returns the smallest of the two values *)
val maxval : tree -> item
(*Pre: takes a 2-3 tree which has a node containing 2 values at its
   root
   Post: returns the largest of the two values *)
val insert : item -> tree -> tree
(*Pre: takes an item and a 2-3 search tree.
   Post: returns a 2-3 search tree with the item inserted in the
   correct position *)
val build : item list -> tree -> tree
(*Pre: takes a list of items and a tree which is empty initially.
   Post: returns a 2-3 search tree with the items inserted in the
   correct positions *)
end
```

The implementing functor is given below. It depends on the type of items in the tree, the implementation of 2-3 trees and the applications functor (containing the function height) which was created earlier, and so its heading includes these as parameters. Pre- and postconditions are included for the functions which are private and so are not listed in the signature (reshape, rebalance and reform).

```
functor MkOrd (structure I : ITEM and T : TREE and A : APPS) : ORD =
struct

  open A        (* applications functor, providing the function height *)
  open T                              (* 2-3 tree access functions *)

fun minval t = if numvals t = 2 then I.min (first t) (second t)
               else hd []

fun maxval t = if numvals t = 2 then I.max (first t) (second t)
               else hd []

(*Pre: reshapes a tree of ht <=3, which has grown due to an
   insertion *)
(*Post: returns a 2-3 search tree *)
fun reshape t = if isempty t then t
                else
                if (numvals t = 1) then
                    if height (left t) = height (right t) then t
                    else
                    if height (left t) > height (right t) then
                        cons2 (root (left t)) (root t) (left (left t))
                                           (right (left t)) (right t)
                    else
                    cons2 (root t) (root (right t)) (left t)  (left
                                      (right t)) (right (right t))
                else
                    if height (left t) = height (middle t) andalso
                           height (middle t) = height (right t) then t
                    else
```

```
                          if  height (left t) > height (right t) andalso
                                  height (left t) > height (middle t) then
                              cons (minval t) (left t)  (cons (maxval t)
                                                     (middle t) (right t))
                          else
                          if  height (middle t) > height (right t) andalso
                                  height (middle t) > height (left t) then
                              cons (root (middle t)) (cons (minval t)
                                              (left t) (left (middle t)))
                                      (cons (maxval t) (right (middle t))
                                                               (right t))
                          else (*right tree has grown *)
                          cons (maxval t) (cons (minval t) (left t)
                                                 (middle t))(right t)

   (*Pre: takes a tree and an integer which is initially 3 *)
   (*Post: returns a 2-3 search tree *)
   fun rebalance t n = if height t <= n then reshape t
                          else
                          if numvals t = 1 then
                              if height (left t) > height (right t) then
                                  rebalance (cons (root t) (rebalance
                                              (left t) n) (right t)) (n+1)
                              else
                              if height (left t) < height (right t) then
                                  rebalance (cons (root t)  (left t)
                                          (rebalance (right t) n)) (n+1)
                              else t (*tree is balanced *)
                          else (*numvals = 2*)
                          if height (left t) > height (right t) andalso
                                  height (left t) > height (middle t) then
                              rebalance (cons2 (minval t) (maxval t)
                                  (rebalance (left t) n) (middle t) (right t))
                                                                     (n+1)
                          else
                          if height (middle t) >  height (left t) andalso
                                  height (middle t)  >  height (right t) then
                              rebalance (cons2 (minval t)(maxval t) (left t)
                                      (rebalance (middle t) n) (right t)) (n+1)
                          else
                          rebalance (cons2 (minval t) (maxval t) (left t)
                                  (middle t) (rebalance  (right t) n))(n+1)

   (*Post: returns a 2-3 search tree *)
   fun reform t = rebalance t 3

   fun insert i t = if isempty t then
                          cons i empty empty
                      else
                      if numvals t = 1 then
                          if isempty (left t) andalso isempty (right t) then
                              cons2 i (root t) empty empty empty
                          else
                          if I.isless i (root t) then
                              reform (cons (root t) (insert i (left t))
                                                               (right t))
```

```
                 else
                     reform (cons (root t) (left t) (insert i
                                                            (right t)))
             else
             if isempty (left t) andalso isempty (right t) then
                 cons (I.mid i (minval t) (maxval t))
                         (cons (I.min (minval t) i) empty empty)
                         (cons (I.max (maxval t) i) empty empty)
             else
             if I.isless i (minval t) then
                 reform (cons2 (minval t) (maxval t)
                             (insert i (left t)) (middle t) (right t))
             else
             if I.isgreater i (minval t) andalso I.isless i
                                                       (maxval t) then
                 reform (cons2 (minval t) (maxval t) (left t)
                                 (insert i (middle t)) (right t))
             else
                 reform (cons2 (minval t) (maxval t)(left t)
                                 (middle t)   (insert i (right t)))

  fun build [] t = t
    | build (x::xs) t = build xs (insert x t)

  end
```

Validation

To validate this implementation, we must provide structures which match the three signatures ITEM, TREE and APPS. For example, to create a 2-3 search tree of integers, we could use a structure with signature ITEM such as the one shown below:

```
structure IntItem : ITEM =
  struct
  type item = int
  fun isequal a b = a = b
  fun isless (a:item) b = a < b
  fun isgreater (a:item) b = a > b
  fun min (a:item) b = if a < b then a else b
  fun max (a:item) b = if a > b then a else b
  fun mid (a:item) b c = if a < max b c andalso a > min b c then a
                         else
                         if b < max a c andalso b > min a c then b
                         else c
  fun key a = a
  (*Post: identity function, unless the items have a search key *)
  fun showitem (a:item) = makestring a
  fun format f xs = output (open_out f, showstring "tree " "" "\n" xs)
  (*Post: opens a file f and outputs the list of strings xs to f,
  using showstring to format the output *)
  end
```

Now we can instantiate the other structures, IntTree and IntApps, as follows:

```
structure IntTree = MkTree (IntItem)
```

```
structure IntApps = MkApplications (structure I = IntItem and T =
                                                   IntTree)
```

and using these structures we can instantiate the MkOrd functor, as follows:

```
structure IntOrd = MkOrd (structure I = IntItem and T = IntTree and
                                        A = IntApps)
```

For example, to insert the value 2 into the tree in Figure 7.8, we could use the statement:

```
format "f" (showtree (insert 2 t))
```

where

```
val t = cons 50 (cons 20 (cons2 7 13 (cons2 1 3 empty empty empty)
                                     (cons2 8 10 empty empty empty)
                         (cons2 14 16 empty empty empty))
                         (cons2 25 40 (cons 21 empty empty)
                         (cons 27 empty empty)(cons 42 empty
                                                       empty)))
                         (cons2 60 70 (cons 55 (cons 53 empty empty)
                                              (cons 57 empty empty))
                         (cons 67 (cons 62 empty empty)
                         (cons 68 empty empty))
                         (cons 80 (cons 75 empty empty)
                         (cons 85 empty empty)))
```

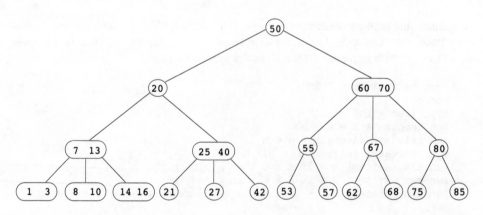

Figure 7.8

This will send the result:

```
tree (50,(7,20,(2,(1),(3)),(13,(8,10),(14,16)),(25,40,(21),(27),(42))),
        (60,70,(55,(53),(57)),(67,(62),(68)),(80,(75),(85))))
```

(which is the tree shown in Figure 7.9) to the file f.

All of the access functions for 2-3 search trees should be extensively tested in this manner.

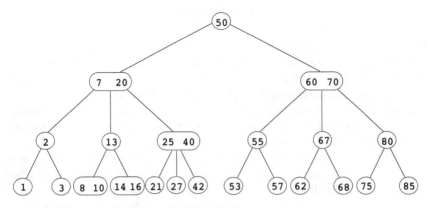

Figure 7.9

EXERCISES 7.2

1. By rewriting, determine the tree which results from the evaluation of the following
expression, using the function insert which was given earlier for 2-3 search trees:

```
insert 2 (cons 20 (cons2 7 13 (cons2 1 3 empty empty empty)
              (cons2 8 10 empty empty empty)
              (cons2 14 16 empty empty empty))
              (cons2 25 40 (cons 21 empty empty)
              (cons 27 empty empty)
              (cons 42 empty empty)))
```

2. Implement the function find, the heading of which is given below:

```
val find : int -> tree -> item
(*Pre: takes an integer key and a 2-3 search tree
   Post: returns the information associated with the key *)
```

3. Write a function which flattens a 2-3 search tree in inorder, so that the resulting list of
items is in ascending order (for example, a 2-3 search tree of characters would be flattened to a list which is in alphabetical order). The function heading is given below:

```
val inorder  : tree -> item list
(*Pre: takes a 2-3 search tree
   Post: returns a list (in ascending order) of the items which are
   in the tree *)
```

4. Specify the following function:

```
val delete : item -> tree -> tree
(*Pre: takes an item and a 2-3 search tree
Post: returns a 2-3 search tree without the specified item *)
```

SUMMARY

- The ADT *2-3 tree* is a finite set of nodes which is either empty, or consists of a root containing one item and two disjoint subtrees, or consists of a root containing two items and three disjoint subtrees, (called left, middle and right), where the subtrees are 2-3 trees of the same height, together with a number of access functions.
- When specifying a 2-3 tree algebraically we can use the specification of a binary tree as a basis and add extra functions to cope with the middle subtree and the fact that the root may contain either one or two items.
- The ADT *2-3 search tree* is a 2-3 tree which has an ordering imposed on the nodes such that, if there is one item at the root, all values in its left subtree are less than the value at the root, and all values in its right subtree are greater than the value at the root, and both subtrees are also 2-3 search trees. Otherwise, if there are 2 items at the root of the tree, the smaller value of the two must be greater than all values in the left subtree and less than all values in the middle subtree, and the larger of the two must be greater than all values in the middle subtree and less than all values in the right subtree. Again all the subtrees must be 2-3 search trees.
- A 2-3 search tree is always perfectly balanced, and the insertion algorithm ensures that if it does grow, it will remain balanced. Consequently, searching such a tree is very efficient ($O(\log_2 n)$, where n is the number of items in the tree).

CHAPTER 8

Sets

INTRODUCTION

In this chapter we discuss the ADT *set*. The type set is provided as a built-in type in some programming languages (such as Modula-2 and Pascal). We give the algebraic specification of the ADT and then discuss possible implementations. We then discuss the abstract data type *multiset*, which differs from the type set in allowing multiple occurrences of an item to be present.

DEFINITION

The ADT *set* is a collection of an arbitrary number of distinct items (all of the same type) together with a number of access functions.

Note the difference between this definition and that of the ADT stack. The items in a stack do not have to be distinct, and they have a linear ordering imposed on them which reflects the order in which the items were inserted into the stack. On the other hand, duplicate items are not allowed in a set, and the order in which items are placed in a set is not significant.

REPRESENTATION AND NOTATION

We will represent a set by listing its members in curly brackets, and show the items in a set separated by commas:

```
{"a", "e", "i", "o", "u"}   : a set of strings
```

The notation used with sets has been inherited from mathematics; for example, we talk about the *union*, *intersection* and *difference* of two sets, and so on. These characteristic functions will be more formally defined as part of the algebraic specification, which is given next.

ALGEBRAIC SPECIFICATION

As usual, we have two constructor functions, which are used to create an empty set and insert an item into a set. We also have two predicate functions, one of which tests a set to see if it is empty, and another which tests a set to see if it contains a named item. We have one selector function which returns a set without a named item. Some auxiliary functions are included here, either because they are fundamental to our concept of the ADT (the functions union, intersection, difference and subset) or, in the case of the function size, because of its practicality.

Syntax of the Access Functions

1. Constructor functions

```
val empty : set
(*Post: returns an empty set *)

val insert : item -> set -> set
(*Pre:  receives an item and a set
   Post: returns a new set which consists all the items of the set and
   the new item, if it was not  already in the set*)
```

2. Predicate functions

```
val isempty : set -> bool
(*Pre: receives a set
   Post: returns true if the set is empty, otherwise false. *)

val isin : item -> set -> bool
(*Pre: receives an item  and a set
   Post: returns true if the item is in the set, otherwise false. *)
```

3. Selector functions

```
val remove : item -> set -> set
(*Pre: receives an item  and a set
   Post: returns a set which contains all the items except the named
   one. *)
```

4. Auxiliary functions

```
val union : set -> set -> set
(*Pre: receives two sets
   Post: returns the set of all items which are either in either one
   set or the other or in both. *)

val intersection : set -> set -> set
(*Pre: receives two sets
   Post: returns the set of all items in the first set which are also
   in the second. *)

val difference : set -> set -> set
(*Pre: receives two sets
   Post: returns the set of all items in the first which are not in the
   second. *)

val subset : set -> set -> bool
(*Pre: receives two sets
   Post: returns true if the first set is a subset of the second. *)
```

```
   val size : set -> int
(*Pre: receives a set
  Post: returns the cardinality of the set *)
```

Semantics of the Access Functions

The access functions should satisfy the following axioms, where i and j are items and s and t are sets. The axioms can be derived by case analysis, using the fact that a set is either empty or has been constructed by inserting an item i into a set s, in which case it is of the form (insert i s). The first axiom specifies that an item i cannot be inserted into a set s if it is already in s. Assuming that a set is represented as a list, we have:

```
1.   insert i s = if (isin i s) then s
                      else
                      i::s
```

The next two axioms describe the behaviour of the predicate function isempty, and are similar to those which we have seen in earlier chapters.

```
2.   isempty empty = true
3.   isempty (insert i s) = false
```

The semantics for the function isin describe how we can determine whether an item is in a set or not. The first axiom states that an item is not contained in the empty set:

```
4.   isin i empty = false
```

If the item which we are checking has just been inserted into the set then isin must return true, otherwise we must determine whether the item was in the original set:

```
5.   isin j (insert i s) = if i = j then true
                      else
                      isin j s
```

Now consider the semantics for the function remove. We will specify this function so that if the item to be removed is not in the set then the original set is returned. This gives us the following axiom if the set is empty:

```
6.   remove i empty = empty
```

If an item i which is about to be inserted into a set is equal to the item j being deleted, then all we need to do is to remove any other occurrence of j from the set (because duplicates are not allowed in the set). So we have:

```
     remove j (insert i s) = if i = j then
                      remove j s
```

Otherwise we still need to insert the item i into the set s, and we also need to remove the item j from the set:

```
     else
     insert i (remove j s)
```

Hence the second axiom describing the semantics for the function remove is given by:

```
7.   remove j (insert i s) = if i = j then
                                  remove j s
                             else
                             insert i (remove j s)
```

Note that if the item j is not in the set s then this would eventually be rewritten to:

```
    remove j empty
```

which (using axiom 6) rewrites to the empty set. For example, the rewriting of the expression:

```
    remove a { f, c, e }
```

proceeds as follows:

```
remove a { f, c, e }    → remove a (insert f {c, e})
                        → insert f (remove a {c, e})
                        → insert f (insert c (remove a {e}))
                        → insert f (insert c (insert e (remove a
                                                          { })))
                        → insert f (insert c (insert e { }))
                        → {f, c, e}
```

Whereas removing an item which is in a set can be demonstrated by rewriting the following expression:

```
    remove a {f, a, e}
```

to normal form:

```
remove a { f, a, e }    → remove a (insert f {a, e} )
                        → insert f (remove a {a, e} )
                        → insert f (remove a {e} )
                        → insert f (insert e (remove a { } ))
                        → insert f (insert e { } )
                        → {f, e}
```

Turning to the auxiliary functions, the function union takes two sets and returns the set of all items which are either in one set or the other or in both. If one set is empty then we simply need to return the other set:

```
8.   union s empty = s
```

If a set is not empty then it must be of the form (insert i t) where t is a set (and hence contains no duplicate items) and i is an item. In this case we simply need to return the result of inserting i into the union of the two sets:

```
9.   union s (insert i t) = insert i (union s t)
```

The function `intersection` takes two sets and returns a set containing all the items which are in both sets. Obviously if one set is empty then the intersection will also be empty:

10. `intersection s empty = empty`

Otherwise we must ask whether an item which is about to be inserted into a set is contained in the other set, in which case it should be inserted into the intersection of the two sets:

```
intersection s (insert i t)  = if (isin i s) then
                                    insert i (intersection s t)
```

and if not then we simply ignore the item and look for the intersection of the sets:

```
else intersection s t
```

which gives us the axiom below:

11. `intersection s (insert i t) = if (isin i s) then`
```
                                        insert i (intersection s t)
                                    else
                                    intersection s t
```

We want to define the difference of two sets to be every item which is in the first set but not in the second. So if the second set is empty then we want the whole of the first set:

12. `difference s empty = s`

Otherwise we follow the axiom for `intersection` except that we *remove* any item which occurs in the second set:

13. `difference s (insert i t) = if (isin i s) then`
```
                                    remove i (difference s t)
                                else
                                difference s t
```

In fact, there is no need to check for the presence of an item in the set, because axiom 7 guarantees that an item is only removed if it is contained in the set, and otherwise the function has no effect. So we can simplify axiom 13 to:

13. `difference s (insert i t) = remove i (difference s t)`

For example, suppose we rewrite the call to the following expression:

```
difference {a,f,c} {a,e}
```

to normal form:

```
difference {a,f,c} {a,e}   →   remove a (difference  {a,f,c} {e})
                           →   remove a (difference { a, f, c }
                                                               { } )
                           →   remove a {a, f, c }
                           →   {f, c}
```

The next two axioms give the semantics of the function for the function subset:

```
14.  subset empty t = true
15.  subset (insert i s) t = if isin i t then
                                  subset s t
                             else false
```

Finally, for the function size, we have the following axioms:

```
16.  size empty = 0
17.  size (insert i s) = 1 + size (remove i s)
```

Note that it is not correct to give axiom 17 as:

```
size (insert i s) = 1 + size s
```

because the item i will not be inserted into the set s if it is already in it (as axiom 1 guarantees).

The access functions given in the specification were chosen because of their functionality. With such a large number of axioms the question of showing that they are sufficiently complete, i.e. that we can determine the behaviour of every function in every possible case, is not trivial. Consistency (that is, determining whether or not any of the axioms contradict each other) is also unsolvable in theory, although the presence of contradictory axioms is relatively easy to observe in practice.

APPLICATIONS

From the specification it can be seen that the ADT set has no structure imposed on it, unlike the ADT stack which has a linear structure. Consequently sets are very general, and have many applications, particularly in the domain of formal specification. However, this generality can mean that sets are sometimes more complicated to manipulate.

Sets are frequently used to represent the attributes that some object may have, and to test a value against a set of acceptable values. Another application is the implementation of the ADT *graph*, which will be discussed in Chapter 9.

The ADT set is a built-in type in some languages. However, the cardinality of such sets is often restricted to be the size of a machine word.

Examples

Consider the set-covering problem (Cormen *et al* 1990): a given set is partitioned into (possibly overlapping) subsets, and the aim is to find which subsets are needed to provide complete coverage of the original set, in such a way that the minimum number of subsets are used. For example, suppose that we have a set of topics which constitute a Computer Science degree, and that these topics are arranged into courses. Some of the topics are covered by more than one course, and we need to determine which courses (if any) can be removed from the degree syllabus whilst maintaining a degree program in which every topic is covered.

This problem is typical of many of the constraint optimisation problems which arise in the real world, and which are studied in operational research. It is not possible to provide an exact solution for all cases; the best we can do is to provide an approximate solution which is not too inefficient.

The way we can do this is to use a greedy approximation algorithm which takes whatever decision looks best at each step.

The top level function will be called cover:

```
val cover :  set -> set list ->  set list
(*Pre: takes a set and a list of subsets
  Post: returns a list of subsets which cover the given set *)
```

If the set is empty then we return an empty list. Otherwise, we must find the subset that has the largest intersection with the given set, and add this to the list of results, whilst calling the function cover again, this time without the chosen subset. This analysis leads to the following function:

```
fun cover s ts  = if isempty s then []
                  else let val t =  (findmax s ts)
                  in
                  (t::(cover (difference s t) ts ))
                  end
```

where the function findmax finds the required subset by forming a list of the intersecting sets and then finding the one with the greatest cardinality:

```
(*Pre: takes a set and a list of sets
  Post: returns the subset which has the largest intersection with the
  given set *)
fun findmax s (t::ts) = let fun formlist x [] = []
                          | formlist x (y::ys) = (intersection x
                                                  y)::(formlist x ys)
                    in
                        maxsize (formlist s (t::ts))
                    end
```

The function findmax is given below:

```
(*Pre: takes a list of sets
  Post: returns the largest *)
fun maxsize ([x]:set list) = x
  | maxsize (x::y::xs) = if (size x) > (size y) then
                            maxsize (x::xs)
                         else maxsize (y::xs)
```

In order to output the resulting list of sets, we will need a display function, which formats each set as a list of strings:

```
val showlist : set list -> string list list
(*Pre: takes a list of sets
  Post: returns a list of lists of strings *)
```

The implementation of this function will be discussed after we have shown how to implement the ADT.

IMPLEMENTATION

We will consider two possible implementations of sets. The first is a simple but inefficient implementation which uses lists. For both implementations, we can reuse our basic signature for items which acts as an interface for type-dependent functions:

```
signature ITEM =
  sig
  eqtype item
  val isequal : item -> item -> bool
  (*Post: returns true if the items are equal *)
  val isless : item -> item -> bool
  (*Post: returns true if the 1st item is smaller than the 2nd *)
  val isgreater : item -> item -> bool
  (*Post: returns true if the 1st item is larger than the 2nd *)
  val showitem : item -> string
  (*Post: a display function which returns a string *)
  val format : string -> string list -> unit
  (*Post: opens a file and outputs a list of strings to it *)
  end
```

We also have the following signature for the ADT set:

```
signature SET =
  sig
  structure I : ITEM
  type set
  val empty : set
  (*Post: returns an empty set *)
  val isempty : set -> bool
  (*Pre: receives a set
    Post: returns true if the set is empty, otherwise false. *)
  val insert : I.item -> set -> set
  (*Pre:  receives an item and a set
    Post: returns a new set which consists of all the items of the set
    and the new item, if it was not  already in the set*)
  val isin : I.item -> set -> bool
  (*Pre: receives an item and a set
    Post: returns true if the item is in the set, otherwise false. *)
  val subset : set -> set -> bool
  (*Pre: receives two sets
    Post: returns true if the first set is a subset of the second. *)
  val remove : I.item -> set -> set
  (*Pre: receives an item  and a set
```

```
        Post: returns a set which contains all the items except the
        named one. *)
      val union : set -> set -> set
      (*Pre: receives two sets
        Post: returns the set of all items which are either in either one
        set or the other or in both. *)
      val intersection : set -> set -> set
      (*Pre: receives two sets
        Post: returns the set of all items in the first set which are also
        in the second. *)
      val difference : set -> set -> set
      (*Pre: receives two sets
        Post: returns the set of all items in the first which are not in
        the second. *)
      val size : set -> int
      (*Pre: receives a set
        Post: returns the cardinality of the set *)
      val showset : set -> string list
      (*Post: formats a set for output *)
    end
```

A Simple Implementation using Lists

We will implement the access functions within a functor called MkSet. The functor heading and the declaration of the type constructor set for this implementation are as follows:

```
functor MkSet (Itemstruct : ITEM) : SET =
struct
structure I = Itemstruct    (*indicates that this item structure is the
                              same as that used in the signature*)

abstype set =  Set of I.item list
```

In order to implement the constructor function empty we use the data constructor Set together with an empty list:

```
val empty = Set []
```

The predicate function isempty simply compares its parameter with an empty list:

```
fun isempty (Set s) = s = []
```

Since the order in which the member values of the set are held is unimportant we can implement insert simply by adding new members to the head of the list. The implementation must reflect the property (stated by axiom 1) that items in the set should be unique. This gives us the following function:

```
fun insert i  (Set s) = if not (isin i (Set s)) then
                              Set (i::s)
                        else
                        Set s
```

The function insert uses the function isin, and as the latter's implementation occurs after the former's, it must be declared using the keyword and. The specification leads us to the function below, in which the isequal function from the ITEM structure is used to compare the item parameter with an item taken from the set.

```
and isin i (Set []) = false
  | isin i (Set (j::s)) = if I.isequal i j then true
                          else isin i (Set s)
```

Alternatively, we could implement this function using the list membership function provided by our library:

```
fun isin i (Set s) = i member s
```

Similarly, using the algebraic specification for the function subset leads us to the following implementation for the function:

```
fun subset (Set []) (Set t) = true
  | subset (Set (s::ss)) (Set t) = if s member t then
                                        subset (Set ss) (Set t)
                                   else
                                   false
```

To implement the function remove, we note from the semantic specification that removing an item from a set is not an error if the item is not there, and so we can use the list difference function, ––, provided by our library of general purpose routines:

```
fun remove i  (Set s) = Set (s––[i])
```

We can use axioms 8 and 9 to guide the implementation of union, leading to the function below:

```
fun union (Set s) (Set []) = Set s
  | union (Set s) (Set (t::ts)) = insert t (union (Set s)(Set ts))
```

and similarly axioms 10 and 11 dictate the implementation method for intersection:

```
fun intersection (Set s) (Set []) = empty
  | intersection (Set s) (Set (t::ts)) = if t member s then
                                             insert t (intersection
                                                       (Set s) (Set ts))
                                         else
                                         intersection (Set s) (Set ts)
```

The semantics of the function difference are given by axioms 12 and 13, and lead to the following function:

```
fun difference (Set []) (Set t) = empty
  | difference  (Set (s::ss)) (Set t) = if s member t then
                                            difference (Set ss) (Set t)
                                        else
                                        insert s (difference (Set ss)
                                                             (Set t))
```

We can implement the function `size` by using the intrinsic function `length` to determine the length of the list:

```
fun size (Set s) = length s
```

Finally, the function `showset` formats an instance of a set as a list of strings:

```
fun showset (Set []) = ""::[]
  | showset (Set (s::ss)) = (I.showitem s):: showset (Set ss)
```

Summary

Although this implementation is simple to produce, the majority of the functions are not very efficient, because of the need to determine whether or not an item is in the set (the asymptotic analysis for the majority of functions is $O(n)$, where n is the number of items in the set).

An Implementation Using Ordered Trees

Our second implementation for this ADT reuses the implementation of the ordered tree ADT. In order to do this, we will create a functor for the set access functions which is parameterised over items and trees. We will have to use a sharing constraint to inform the system that the items used by sets and those used by ordered trees are of the same type. The functor heading is thus:

```
functor MkSet (structure I: ITEM
               and T : TREE
               sharing type I.item = T.I.item ) : SET =
struct
structure I = I    (*indicates that this item structure is the same as
                    that used in the signature*)
```

We can now implement the type set as a tree:

```
abstype set =  Set of  T.tree
```

The access functions listed in the signature for `MkSet` can be implemented by reusing those for ordered trees. For example:

```
val empty = Set  T.empty

fun isempty (Set s) = T.isempty s

fun insert i  (Set s) = if not (isin i (Set s)) then
                            Set (T.insert i s)
                        else
                            Set s
```

The function `isin` can be implemented by searching either the left or the right subtree, depending on the value being sought:

```
and isin i (Set s) = if T.isempty s then false
                     else
                     if I.isequal (T.root s) i then true
                     else
                     if I.isless i (T.root s) then
                         isin i (Set (T.left s))
                     else
                     isin i (Set (T.right s))
```

The function subset returns true if the first set is empty. Otherwise, the set is decomposed into an item (which is the root of the tree that represents the set) and two sets (which correspond to the left and right subtrees), both of which must be shown to be contained within the second set:

```
fun subset (Set x) (Set y) = if T.isempty x then true
                             else
                             if isin (T.root x) (Set y) then
                                 subset (Set (T.left x)) (Set y)
                                     andalso  subset (Set (T.right x))
                                                                 (Set y)
                             else
                             false
```

To remove an item from the set, we can reuse the function to remove an item from an ordered tree:

```
fun remove i  (Set s) = Set (T.remove i s)
```

The function union must also use the tree selector functions to manipulate the set as a tree, inserting the root of the tree into the resulting set and also forming the union of the two subtrees:

```
fun union (Set x) (Set y) = if T.isempty x then (Set y)
                            else
                            union (union (Set (T.left x))
                                                       (Set (T.right x)))
                                       (insert (T.root x) (Set y))
```

The function intersection can be implemented using the tree access functions and the function union:

```
fun intersection (Set x) (Set y)
    = if T.isempty x then
          empty
      else
      if isin (T.root x) (Set y) then
          insert (T.root x) (union (intersection (Set (T.left x)) (Set y))
                      (intersection (Set (T.right x)) (Set y)))
      else
      (union (intersection (Set (T.left x)) (Set y))
                      (intersection (Set (T.right x)) (Set y)))
```

And similarly for the function `difference`:

```
fun difference (Set x) (Set y)
   = if T.isempty x then
         empty
       else
       if isin (T.root x) (Set y) then
                   union (difference (Set (T.left x)) (Set y))
                         (difference (Set (T.right x)) (Set y))
       else
       insert (T.root x) (union  (difference (Set (T.left x)) (Set y))
               (difference (Set (T.right x)) (Set y)))
```

The function `size` must count the item at the root, and also the items in the left and right subtrees:

```
fun size (Set s) = if T.isempty s then 0
                   else
                   1 + size (Set (T.left s)) + size (Set (T.right s))
```

Finally, the function showset can be implemented by reusing the showtree function:

```
fun showset (Set s) =  T.showtree s
```

The ordered tree implementation uses a function called `incfreq`, the heading of which is given within the item signature. Consequently the item signature for sets will also need to include this function, which can be implemented as the identity function if the items in the set do not have an associated frequency.

Summary

The diagram in Figure 8.1 summarises the way in which the set ADT has been constructed by reusing the ordered tree implementation, and how implementation independent functions can be built on top of the underlying software.

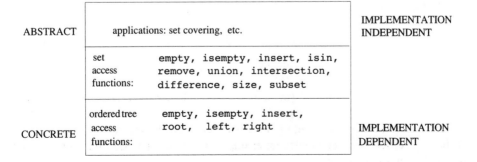

ABSTRACT	applications: set covering, etc.		IMPLEMENTATION INDEPENDENT
	set access functions:	empty, isempty, insert, isin, remove, union, intersection, difference, size, subset	
CONCRETE	ordered tree access functions:	empty, isempty, insert, root, left, right	IMPLEMENTATION DEPENDENT

Figure 8.1

Comparing the ordered tree implementation with the previous one, it is clear that the linear search for membership has been replaced by a binary search, with a resulting improvement in efficiency. Consequently, the function isin now has a time complexity of $O(\log_2 n)$ for a set of n items, as does the function remove. Since isin is used to implement a number of the other functions this improvement may well be significant as n increases. Also, some of the functions have the potential for parallel evaluation, which may be an advantage if the intention is to use a parallel language implementation.

Verification and Validation

We can verify the implementations against the algebraic specification by rewriting calls to the predicate, selector and auxiliary functions with both an empty set and an arbitrary instance of a set. The first implementation is slightly more straightforward to verify than the second, because of the way that it directly reflects the algebraic specification.

Before we can test the implementations, we will have to instantiate the implementing functors. We could provide a structure for integer items, such as the one that follows:

```
structure IntItem : ITEM =
  struct
  type item = int
  fun isequal a b = a = b
  fun isless (a:item) b = a < b
  fun isgreater (a:item) b = a > b
  fun showitem (a:item) = makestring a
  fun format f xs = output (open_out f, showstring "set{" " " "}\n"
                                                                      xs)
  (*Post: opens a file f and outputs the list of strings xs to f,
     using showstring to format the output *)
  fun incfreq a = a              (* needed for compatibility with
                                      ordered tree implementation *)
  end
```

For the first implementation, we can instantiate the MkSet functor by using this structure:

```
structure IntSet = MkSet (IntItem)
```

However, for the ordered tree implementation, we first need to instantiate the MkOrdTree functor:

```
structure IntOrdTree = MkOrdTree (IntItem)
```

after which we can also instantiate the MkSet functor:

```
structure IntSet = MkSet (structure I = IntItem and T = IntOrdTree)
```

We can now validate the access functions for each of the implementations, using the algebraic specification as an oracle. For example, to validate the insert function, we could use a statement of the form:

```
showset (insert 4 s)
```

where:

```
val s = insert 0 (insert 2 (insert 7 (insert 9 (insert 3 (insert 1
                                      (insert 2 (insert 4 empty)))))))
```

to obtain the result:

```
["0","7","9","3","1","2","4"] : string list
```

which corresponds to the result predicted by axiom 1. With the second implementation, this would be tested by using the statement:

```
format "f" (showset (insert 4 s))
```

which results in the expression:

```
set {((((0),1),2,(3)),4,((7),9))}
```

being sent to the file f.

Applying the Generic ADT

The functions which use the ADT can be implemented within a functor which is constrained by a signature, such as the following:

```
signature APPS =
  sig
  structure S : SET
  open S
  val cover :  set ->  set list ->  set list
  (*Pre: takes a set and a list of subsets
    Post: returns a list of subsets which cover the given set *)
  val showlist : set list -> string list list
  (*Pre: takes a list of sets
    Post: returns a list of lists of strings *)
end
```

The functor itself will take two structures as parameters, one of type ITEM and the other of type SET. A possible outline of the applications functor, containing the function showlist, is shown below:

```
functor MkApplications (structure I : ITEM and S: SET) : APPS =
struct
structure S = S

open S

fun showlist [] = []
  | showlist (x::xs) = (showset x)::showlist xs

  (*remaining body of functor ... *)

end
```

Note that the line:

```
structure S = S
```

is needed because the constraining signature also specifies the use of such a structure.

The MkApplications functor can now be instantiated using the IntItem and IntSet structures:

```
structure IntApps = MkApplications (structure I = IntItem and S =
                                                               IntSet)
```

and used to provide solutions to the set-covering problem, and so on.

MULTISETS

This section considers a variation on the ADT set, called a *multiset*, or *bag*.

Definition

The ADT *multiset* is a collection of an arbitrary number of items (all of the same type) which are *not necessarily distinct* together with a number of access functions.

The specification of the ADT multiset is given in the following section.

Algebraic Specification

Syntax

```
signature MSET =
  sig
  structure I : ITEM
  type mset
  val empty : mset
  (*Post: returns an empty multiset *)
  val isempty : mset -> bool
  (*Pre: receives a multiset
    Post: returns true if the multiset is empty, otherwise false *)
  val insert : I.item -> mset -> mset
  (*Pre:  receives an item and a multiset
    Post: returns a new multiset which consists of all the items of
    the multiset and the new item*)
  val isin : I.item -> mset -> bool
  (*Pre: receives an item  and a multiset
    Post: returns true if the item is in the multiset, otherwise
    false *)
  val subset : mset -> mset -> bool
  (*Pre: receives two multisets
    Post: returns true if the first multiset is a subset of the
    second *)
```

```
      val remove : I.item -> mset -> mset
      (*Pre: receives an item  and a multiset
        Post: returns a multiset which contains all the items except the
        named one *)
      val union : mset -> mset -> mset
      (*Pre: receives two multisets
        Post: returns the multiset of all items which are either in either
        one multiset or the other or in both, including repetitions *)
      val intersection : mset -> mset -> mset
      (*Pre: receives two multisets
        Post: returns the multiset of all items in the first multiset
        which are also in the second, including repetitions*)
      val difference : mset -> mset -> mset
      (*Pre: receives two sets
        Post: returns the multiset of all items in the first which are not
        in the second *)
      val size : mset -> int
      (*Pre: receives a multiset
        Post: returns the cardinality of the multiset *)
      val showmset : mset -> string list
      (*Post: formats a multiset for output  *)
   end
```

Semantics

The semantics for the access functions are given below, where i and j are items, ms and ns are multisets.

Note that the axiom for the function insert, given for the ADT set:

```
1.    insert i s = if (isin i s) then s
                     else
                     i::s
```

is no longer needed, as there are no longer any restrictions on insertion.

The first four axioms are identical to axioms 2 to 5 for the ADT set:

```
1.    isempty empty = true
2.    isempty  (insert i ms) = false
3.    isin i empty  = false
4.    isin j (insert i ms) = if i = j then true
                                else
                                isin j ms
```

The semantics for the function remove must be changed to reflect the fact that multiple occurrences of items are allowed, and the function should only remove one instance of an item.

```
5.    remove i empty = empty
6.    remove j (insert i ms) = if i = j then ms
                                  else
                                  insert i (remove j ms)
```

When forming the union of two multisets, we want the multiplicity (the number of occurrences) of an item in the resulting multiset to be equal to its total multiplicity in both of the multisets. For example,

```
union { a, c, b } { a, e, d, c, a } = {a, c, b, a, e, d, c, a}
```

Because the semantics of `insert` have now changed, the specification for this function is the same as it was previously:

```
7.    union ms empty = ms
8.    union ms (insert i ns) = insert i (union ms ns)
```

For intersection, we want the multiplicity of an item in the intersection of two multisets to be equal to its least multiplicity in either multiset. So, for example:

```
intersection  { a, c, b } { a, e, d, c, a }  = {a, c}
```

Consequently, the axiom for intersection with a non-empty set must be changed to reflect this:

```
9.    intersection ms empty = empty
10.   intersection ms (insert i ns) = if (isin i ms) then
                                        insert i (intersection (remove
                                                                 i ms) ns)
                         else
                         intersection ns ms
```

The axioms for `difference` remain the same, as do those for `subset`:

```
11.   difference ms empty = ms
12.   difference ms (insert i ns) = remove i (difference ms ns)
13.   subset empty ms = true
14.   subset (insert i ms) ns = if isin i ns then
                                  subset ms ns
                       else false
```

Finally, the second axiom for the function `size` is slightly simpler:

```
15.   size empty = 0
16.   size (insert i ms) = 1 + size   ms
```

The implementation of the access functions is left as an exercise for the reader.

EXERCISE 8.1

1. Provide an efficient implementation for the ADT multiset.

SUMMARY

- The ADT *set* is a collection of an arbitrary number of distinct items (of the same type) together with a number of access functions.
- Duplicate items are not allowed in a set, and there is no ordering imposed on the items in a set.
- Sets are very general, and have many applications, particularly in the domain of formal specification.
- In the set-covering problem a given set is partitioned into (possibly overlapping) subsets, and the aim is to find which subsets are needed to provide complete coverage of the original set, in such a way that the minimum number of subsets are used.
- We have demonstrated the implementation of a set using lists (which gives functions with time complexity of $O(n)$, for n items) and ordered trees (which yields functions with a complexity of $O(\log_2 n)$).
- The abstract data type *multiset* is a collection of an arbitrary number of items (all of the same type) which are *not necessarily distinct* together with a number of access functions.

CHAPTER 9

Graphs

INTRODUCTION

The binary tree ADT is non-linear, in that each item may have as many as two successors, although no more than one predecessor. The ADT *graph* is also a non-linear ADT, and is more general than a binary tree because each item may have zero or more successors and predecessors. In this chapter we introduce some terminology associated with graphs and give an algebraic specification of the ADT. We demonstrate the application of the access functions in the development of functions for searching and sorting graphs, and present a possible implementation of the ADT.

DEFINITION

The ADT *graph* consists of a finite set of nodes and a set of edges, where an edge is a connection between two nodes, together with a number of access functions.

A *directed graph*, or *digraph*, is defined to be a graph in which each edge has a direction. We will assume that the graphs discussed in this chapter are directed and omit the term *directed*.

Before we give the algebraic specification of the ADT graph we will introduce some of the terminology which has come to be associated with it.

REPRESENTATION AND NOTATION

Diagrammatically an edge is shown as a line between two nodes. For each edge of a directed graph one node is said to be the *source* node and the other the *destination* node, and an arrow is drawn from the source node to the destination node. For example, Figure 9.1 shows a digraph of integers.

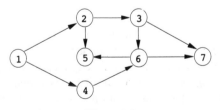

Figure 9.1

175

The source node is said to *precede* the destination node, and the destination node *succeeds* the source node.

If the graph consists of two or more disjoint sets of nodes then it is said to be *disconnected*, otherwise it is said to be *connected*. Figure 9.2 shows examples of both sorts of graphs.

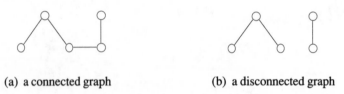

(a) a connected graph   (b) a disconnected graph

Figure 9.2

The word *vertex* is sometimes used instead of *node* and *arc* may be used instead of *edge*.

Two nodes are said to be *adjacent*, or *neighbours*, if there is an edge connecting them. Nodes which are adjacent may be represented by a tuple (a,b) where a and b are the values of the nodes. Examples of some of the adjacent nodes in Figure 9.1 include 1 and 2, 1 and 4, and 6 and 7.

A *path* is a sequence of nodes $n_1, n_2, ..., n_m$ such that for all i from 1 to $(m-1)$, each pair of nodes (n_i, n_{i+1}) are adjacent. In Figure 9.1 there is a path from node 1 to each of the other nodes, but there are no paths starting from node 7.

A path is *simple* if each of its nodes occurs only once in the sequence. (For example, all of the paths given in Figure 9.1 are simple.) A *cycle* is a path that is simple except that the first and last nodes are the same.

If a path from a node to itself does not contain any other nodes then it is said to be a *degenerate cycle*.

A node n_1 is *reachable* from a node n_2 if and only if there exists a path from n_2 to n_1. For each node of a graph there exists a set of nodes which can be reached from that node called the *reachable set*. Thus, a function called reachable which takes a node and returns the set of nodes which are reachable from it would produce the following results for the digraph in Figure 9.1:

```
reachable 1 = {1,2,3,4,5,6,7}
reachable 2 = {2,3,5,6,7}
reachable 3 = {3,5,6,7}
reachable 4 = {4,5,6,7}
reachable 5 = {5}
reachable 6 = {5,6,7}
reachable 7 = {7}
```

A node n_1 is *directly* reachable from a node n_2 if and only if the two nodes are adjacent and n_1 is the successor of n_2. For example, in Figure 9.1 the node 5 is directly reachable only from node 2 and node 6. Node 4 is only directly reachable from node 1.

A digraph is *strongly connected* if and only if for each node in the graph there is at least one path to each of the other nodes. Thus the digraph in Figure 9.1 is connected but not strongly connected.

ALGEBRAIC SPECIFICATION

The algebraic specification comprises of constructor functions to create an empty graph and add an edge to a graph; and three predicate functions which test whether a graph is empty, whether a node is in a graph and whether or not two nodes are adjacent. The specification also provides a selector function which will return a graph without a particular edge, and one which returns the nodes which are adjacent to a given node. We will also need selector functions which return the source and destination nodes of the graph. The following specification assumes that the nodes in the graph are of type node.

Syntax of the Access Functions

1. Constructor functions

```
val empty :  graph
(*Post: returns an empty graph *)

val addedge : edge -> graph -> graph
(*Post: addedge will only  add an edge if it's not already in the
  graph *)
```

2. Predicate functions

```
val isempty :  graph -> bool
(*Post: returns true if the graph is empty, otherwise false *)

val isin : edge ->  graph -> bool
(*Post: returns true if the edge is in the graph, otherwise false *)

val contains :  graph -> node -> bool
(*Post: returns true if the node is in the graph, otherwise false *)
```

3. Selector functions

```
val delete_edge : edge ->  graph ->  graph
(*Post: deletes the given edge if it's present, otherwise it has no
  effect *)

val adj : node ->  graph -> node list
(*Post: returns a list of the nodes which are directly reachable from
  the given node *)

val sources :  graph -> node list
(*Post: returns the set of nodes from which edges emanate *)

val dests :  graph -> node list
(*Post: returns the set of nodes which edges finish at *)
```

Note that the specification allows for graphs which may be disconnected.

Semantics of the Access Functions

The access functions must satisfy the following axioms, where g is a graph, e1 and e2 are edges and m, n, p and q are nodes. An edge may be denoted by a pair of nodes, (n, m), where necessary. The axioms are constructed by case analysis: a graph is either empty, or has been constructed using the function addedge, and so is of the form (addedge el g).

The following two axioms give the semantics of isempty:

1.   isempty empty = true

2.   isempty (addedge e g) = false

The next axiom states that we cannot add an edge to a graph if it is already in the graph, to ensure that there are no duplicate edges:

3.   addedge el g = if (isin el g) then g
                        else
                        addedge el g

The following axioms describe the behaviour of the function contains for each form of graph:

4.   contains empty n = false

5.   contains (addedge (n, m) g) p = if p = n or p = m then true
                                         else
                                         contains g p

The following axioms give the behaviour of isin. The first axiom states that an edge is not present in an empty graph:

6.   isin el empty = false

If a graph has been formed by the addition of an edge, then we must check to see if the edge is the one we are interested in and return *true* if it is. Otherwise we ask whether the edge existed in the graph before the new edge was added:

7.   isin el (addedge e2 g) = if el = e2 then
                                      true
                               else
                               isin el g

Note that two edges are only equal if both their source nodes and their destination nodes are the same; for graphs which are not directed we would need to compare the individual nodes for equality.

Our next two axioms describe the behaviour of delete_edge. We cannot delete an edge from an empty graph:

8.   delete_edge el empty = empty

If an edge which is equal to the edge to be deleted were about to be added to a graph, then the addition does not take place. We may still need to delete the edge from the graph:

```
delete_edge  e1 (addedge e2 g) = if e1 = e2 then
                                        delete_edge  e1 g
```

Otherwise the addition can take place, and the edge must still be deleted from the graph:

```
else addedge e2 (delete_edge  e1 g)
```

This gives us axiom 9:

```
9.   delete_edge  e1 (addedge e2 g) = if e1 = e2 then
                                            delete_edge  e1 g
                                      else
                                      addedge e2 (delete_edge  e1 g)
```

For the function adj, we have the following specification:

```
10.   adj n empty = []
11.   adj n (addedge (p, q) g) = if n = p then
                                       q :: adj n g
                                 else
                                 adj n g
```

The final selector functions, sources and dests, have very similar specifications:

```
12.   sources empty = []
13.   sources (addedge (n, m) g) = n :: sources g
14.   dests empty = []
15.   dests (addedge (n, m) g) = m :: dests g
```

From this specification of the ADT graph we can see that the edges in the graph must be unique.

The access functions were chosen because of the operations which they enable us to perform. We have constructor functions which allow us to create an empty graph and insert edges into a graph. The selector functions enable us to select parts of a graph and the predicate functions enable us to obtain certain information from a graph.

APPLICATIONS

The graph ADT is an extension of the binary tree ADT, which in turn is a extension of the stack ADT. (Note that a tree is an *acyclic* graph, i.e. a graph which does not have any cycles.) Because of its generality the ADT graph has a wide variety of applications, from the representation of chip circuit diagrams, to the simulation and optimisation of constraint networks (such as flight paths) and the implementation of functional languages, to name but a few.

Example

A project is made up of a number of separate activities, some of which must be completed before others can start. If the time that each activity will take is known then the latest

completion date for the entire project can be calculated. A *critical path* is a path from the
start to the end of a project such that if any activity on it is delayed by an amount T, then
the entire project is delayed by T. The interactions between activities may be expressed as
a directed graph. For example, during the production of a software system we could
utilise the digraph in Figure 9.3.

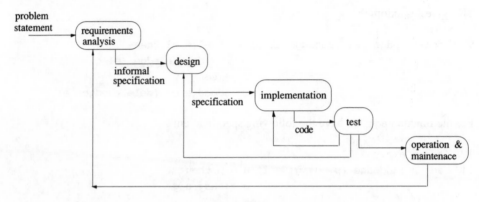

Figure 9.3

We will use the access functions to implement three graph manipulation algorithms,
two for searching and one for sorting. All of these algorithms are potentially non-deter-
ministic, in that there may be more than one way to process the nodes in the digraph.
However, the implementations of the algorithms are all deterministic: each function will
always produce the same answer, given the same arguments.

The hierarchy of software components for manipulation of the ADT graph is illustrated
in Figure 9.4.

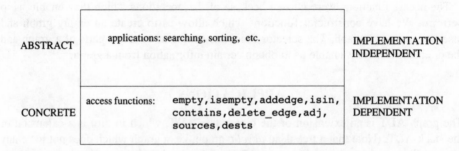

Figure 9.4

Searching

The two searching algorithms provide us with methods to traverse graphs, and so can be
considered to be extensions of the tree traversal algorithms. The aim is to visit each node
which can be reached from a particular starting node exactly once.

Depth first search

A depth first search of a graph starts by processing all of the nodes which are on a path from a given starting node. When a node is reached which has no adjacent nodes, or whose adjacent nodes have all been processed, the algorithm backtracks to the last node visited which still has a neighbour to be processed, and a depth first search is started from there. Finally, we reach a point where no more nodes can be reached from any of the processed nodes.

For example, depth first traversals for the graph in Figure 9.5, starting at the node labelled 1, include the following:

    1 2 3 6 5 7 4

and

    1 2 3 6 7 5 4

and

    1 2 3 7 6 5 4

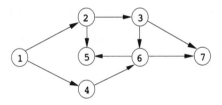

Figure 9.5

Note that if the digraph is not strongly connected, then a depth first search may not visit all of the nodes. For example, possible depth first traversals, starting at the node labelled 2, include:

    2 3 6 5 7

and

    2 3 7 6 5

and starting at the node labelled 3, we have:

    3 6 5 7

and:

    3 6 7 5

and so on. An informal specification of the functions is given below:

```
val depth  :  node list -> graph -> node list -> node list
(*Pre: takes a list with the start node in it, a graph and an
   accumulating parameter which is initially empty
   Post: returns a list of nodes, produced by a depth first traversal
   of the graph from the start node *)
```

To implement the algorithm, we will use an accumulating parameter to store the nodes which have been visited (the parameter acc in the function depth, given below). Initially, the list represented by (x::xs) consists of the node with which we wish to start the traversal: each time the function is called, this list is augmented by the nodes which are adjacent to x, until finally no more nodes are reachable. We use append, @, to add the nodes to the accumulating parameter so that the final result is in the correct order, and the function member, supplied as part of our library of utility functions, to check for membership of the accumulating list.

```
fun depth [] g acc = acc
  | depth (x::xs) g acc = if x member acc then
                              depth xs g acc
                          else
                              depth ((adj x g)@xs) g (acc@[x])
```

For example, we can perform a depth first search for the graph shown in Figure 9.5, starting from the node labelled 1, with the following expression :

```
depth [1] (addedge (1,2) (addedge (1,4) (addedge (2,3) (addedge (2,5)
    (addedge (3,6) (addedge (3,7) (addedge (4,6) (addedge (6,5)
    (addedge (6, 7) empty)))))))))  []
```

to obtain the result:

```
[1,2,3,6,5,7,4] : node list
```

In order to visit *all* of the nodes in a graph in a depth first search, we must incorporate the function depth into a more general function, such as the function dfs shown below. This uses a local function, dfs', which calls the function depth for each node in the graph:

```
val dfs : graph -> node list list
(*Pre: takes a graph
   Post: returns a list of lists of nodes, produced by a depth first
   traversal of the entire graph *)

fun dfs g = let val (s::ss) = sources g
            in let fun dfs' g (s::ss) = depth [s] g []::dfs' g ss
                      | dfs' g [] = []
               in dfs' g (s::ss)
               end
            end
```

For example, for the graph shown in Figure 9.5 we may obtain the following list of lists of nodes:

```
[[1,2,3,6,5,7,4],[2,3,6,5,7],[3,6,5,7],[4,6,5,7],[6,5,7]]
```

Breadth first search

A breadth first search of a graph finds all of the nodes which are adjacent to a given starting node, then finds all of the nodes which are adjacent to one of the processed nodes,
and so on.

For example, for the graph shown in Figure 9.5, possible breadth first searches, starting
at the node labelled 1, include:

```
1 2 4 5 3 6 7
```

and

```
1 4 2 5 3 6 7
```

The informal specification of the function is given below:

```
val breadth :   node list -> graph -> node list -> node list
(*Pre: takes a list with the start node in it, a graph and an
   accumulating parameter which is initially empty
   Post: returns a list of nodes, produced by a breadth first traversal
   of the graph from the start node *)
```

We can derive the breadth first algorithm from the function depth: the only change
necessary is to append the nodes to be visited to the end of the list of waiting nodes,
rather than inserting them at the front of the list to be processed first. This has the desired
effect of ensuring that all nodes adjacent to a particular starting node are processed before
any other nodes.

```
fun breadth [] g acc = acc
  | breadth (x::xs) g acc = if x  member acc then
                            breadth xs g acc
                            else
                            breadth (xs@(adj x g)) g (acc@[x])
```

Note that the breadth first algorithm effectively uses a queue to hold the waiting items,
whereas the depth first algorithm uses a stack.

Sorting

Topological sort

A topological sort provides us with a sorting technique for graphs, and produces a sorted
list such that if there exists an edge from v to w, then v precedes w in the sorted list.

The sort operates by finding a node with no incoming edges. This node is added to the
output list and then the rest of the graph (without the node and any edges which were
attached to it) is topologically sorted.

However, it is easier to find a list of source nodes in a digraph than it is to find the
node with fewest incoming edges, and so this is how our algorithm is implemented.
Again, we use an accumulating parameter (which acts as a stack) to store the sorted
nodes, and the function is called recursively until there are no more nodes with predecessors.

We can specify the algorithm in pseudocode, as shown below:

```
val topsort :  graph -> node list
(*Pre: takes a graph
  Post : returns a sorted list of nodes *)
```

```
find a list of nodes which are source nodes
for this list do
    if the list is empty, then return the accumulating parameter
    else
    check the 1st item in the list
    if it is in the accumulating parameter then
        ignore it and consider the rest of the list
    else add it to the accumulating parameter, and also add all the
        nodes which are reached by doing a topological sort from all of
        its adjacent nodes
```

For example, the source nodes (given by the function sources) for the graph in Figure 9.5 are: 1, 2, 3, 4, and 6, and possible topological sorts are:

```
1 4 2 3 6 7 5
1 2 4 3 6 5 7
1 4 2 3 6 5 7
1 2 4 3 6 7 5
```

The function topsort is given below, translated from the pseudocode into SML:

```
fun topsort g = tsort (sources g) [] g
```

where the auxiliary function tsort is given by:

```
(*Pre: takes a list of nodes and an accumulating parameter which is
  empty initially
  Post : returns a sorted list of nodes *)
fun tsort [] acc g = acc
  | tsort (x::xs) acc g = if (x member acc) then
                                  tsort xs acc g
                          else
                          tsort xs (x::(tsort (adj x g) acc g)) g
```

Consider topologically sorting the graph below (which is equivalent to the graph in Figure 9.5):

```
val g = addedge (1,2) (addedge (1,4) (addedge (2,3) (addedge (2,5)
            (addedge (3,6) (addedge (3,7) (addedge (4,6) (addedge (6,5)
            (addedge (6,7) empty))))))))
```

The rewrite to normal form of a call to topsort proceeds as follows:

```
topsort g  →   tsort (sources g) [] g
           →   tsort [1,2,3,4,6] [] g
           →   tsort [2,3,4,6] (1::tsort [2,4] [] g) g            (1)
```

Now,

```
tsort [2,4] [] g  →  tsort [4] (2::(tsort [3,5] [] g) g)          (2)
```

and

$$\text{tsort } [3,5] \; [] \; g \; \rightarrow \; \text{tsort } [5] \; (3::(\text{tsort } [6,7] \; [] \; g) \; g \qquad\qquad (3)$$

and

$$\text{tsort } [6,7] \; [] \; g \; \rightarrow \; \text{tsort } [7] \; (6:: \; \text{tsort } [5,7] \; [] \; g) \; g \qquad\qquad (4)$$

and

```
tsort [5,7] [] g  →   tsort [7] (5::(tsort [] [] g)) g
                  →   tsort [7] [5] g
                  →   tsort [] 7::(tsort [] [5] g) g
                  →   tsort [] 7::[5] g
                  →   [7,5]
```

∴ from 4,

```
tsort [6,7] [] g  →  tsort [7] [6,7,5] g
                  →   [6,7,5]
```

∴ from 3,

```
tsort [3,5] [] g  →  tsort [5] [3,6,7,5] g
                  →  tsort [] [3,6,7,5] g
                  →  [3,6,7,5]
```

∴ from 2,

```
tsort [2,4] [] g  →  tsort [4] [2,3,6,7,5] g
                  →  tsort [] [4,2,3,6,7,5] g
                  →  [4,2,3,6,7,5]
```

∴ from 1,

```
topsort g         →  tsort [2,3,4,6]  [1,4,2,3,6,7,5] g
                  →   [1,4,2,3,6,7,5]
```

IMPLEMENTATION

The functions which manipulate the nodes in the graph will be implemented within a structure with a constraining signature. We need to be able to compare two nodes for equality, so the type representing nodes must be an equality type, and we must provide an isequal function. If we want to be able to display the contents of nodes then we must provide a function to do this (a function shownodes, say). If each edge is formatted as a string containing a pair of nodes, then in order to display a graph we will also need a formatting function which we can use to send the list of strings to a file. These considerations lead us to the following signature for nodes:

```
signature NODE =
  sig
  eqtype node
```

```
        val isequal : node -> node -> bool
        (*Post: returns true if the nodes are equal *)
        val shownodes : node * node -> string
        (*Post: a display function which returns a string *)
        val format : string -> string list -> unit
        (*Post: opens a file and outputs a list of strings to it *)
    end
```

We will also define the signature for the ADT graph:

```
signature GRAPH =
    sig
    structure N : NODE
    open N
    type edge
    type  graph
    val empty  :  graph
    (*Post: returns an empty graph *)
    val isempty   :  graph -> bool
    (*Post: returns true if the graph is empty, otherwise false *)
    val addedge   : edge ->  graph ->  graph
    (*Post: addedge will only  add an edge if it's not already in the
    graph *)
    val isin   : edge ->  graph -> bool
    (*Post: isin checks to see if the edge is in the graph *)
    val adj   : node ->  graph -> node list
    (*Post: returns a list of the nodes which are directly reachable
    from the given node *)
    val delete_edge   : edge ->  graph ->  graph
    (*Post: deletes the given edge if it's present, otherwise it has no
    effect *)
    val contains   :  graph -> node -> bool
    (*Post: returns true if the node is in the graph, otherwise false *)
    val sources   :  graph -> node list
    (*Post: returns the set of nodes from which edges emanate *)
    val dests   :  graph -> node list
    (*Post: returns the set of nodes which edges finish at *)
    val showgraph   :  graph -> string list
    (*Post:  formats a graph for output to a text stream *)
    end
```

Now we can declare a functor, MkGraph, which defines a structure with signature
GRAPH which takes a parameter Nodestruct with signature NODE, as shown below. The
type graph is implemented as a list of edges.

```
functor MkGraph (Nodestruct: NODE) : GRAPH =
struct
structure N = Nodestruct    (*for compatibility with the signature
                              GRAPH*)

type edge = N.node * N.node

abstype graph = Graph of edge list
```

The functions empty and isempty are straightforward to implement:

```
val empty = Graph []

fun isempty (Graph g) = g = []
```

The functions addedge and isin use the auxiliary library function member (which checks for list membership):

```
fun addedge e (Graph g) = if not (e member g) then
                                Graph (e::g)
                          else Graph g

fun isin e (Graph g) = e member g
```

The implementation of the function adj reflects its algebraic specification:

```
fun adj n (Graph []) = []
  | adj n (Graph ((x,y)::gs)) = if N.isequal n x then
                                   (y::(adj n (Graph gs)))
                                else adj n (Graph gs)
```

The function delete_edge makes use of our standard library functions member and −− (list difference):

```
fun delete_edge e (Graph g) = if e member g then
                                 Graph (g −− [e])
                              else  Graph g
```

The predicate function contains finds all the source and destination nodes, using our library functions fsts and snds, which take a list of pairs and return a list of the first and second items (respectively) in the pairs:

```
fun contains (Graph g) n = n member (fsts g) orelse n member (snds g)
```

The functions sources and dests can also be implemented using these library functions:

```
fun sources (Graph g) = mkset (fsts g)

fun dests (Graph g) =  mkset (snds g)
```

Finally, the function showgraph is shown below:

```
fun showgraph (Graph ((a,b)::gs)) =  if (gs = []) then
                                        (N.shownodes (a,b))::[]
                                     else
                                        (N.shownodes (a,b)) ^ " " ::
                                                (showgraph (Graph gs))
  | showgraph (Graph []) = ""::[]
```

Validation

To instantiate the functor MkGraph we must provide structures of type NODE. Below is a structure in which the nodes are of type integer. The function shownodes formats nodes as strings surrounded by brackets. The function format uses an auxiliary function show-string, which separates strings in a list by chosen characters: here, we choose to start the output with the word graph followed by an opening brace, and to place a closing brace at each end of the graph.

```
structure IntNode : NODE =
  struct
  type node = int
  fun isequal a b = a = b
  fun shownodes ((a:node),(b:node)) = "(" ^ makestring a ^ "," ^
                                            makestring b ^ ")"
  fun format f xs = output (open_out f, showstring "graph{" " " "}\n"
                                                                xs)
  (*Post: opens a file f and outputs the list of strings xs to f,
     using showstring to format the output *)

  end
```

We can instantiate the structure IntGraph by passing the structure IntNode as a parameter to the functor MkGraph:

```
structure IntGraph = MkGraph (IntNode)
```

Now if we open IntGraph and IntNode, and evaluate:

```
format "f" (showgraph g)
```

where:

```
val g = addedge (1,2) (addedge (1,4) (addedge (2,3) (addedge (2,5)
         (addedge (3,6) (addedge (3,7) (addedge (4,6) (addedge (6,5)
         (addedge (6,7) empty))))))))
```

we will find that the file f contains the expression:

```
graph{(1,2) (1,4) (2,3) (2,5) (3,6) (3,7) (4,6) (6,5) (6,7)}
```

which represents the graph in Figure 9.5.

However, if the items in the nodes are of type string, we need to provide an alternative structure, such as the one shown below:

```
structure StringNode : NODE =
  struct
  type node = string
  fun isequal a b = a = b
  fun shownodes ((a:node),(b:node)) = "(" ^ a ^ "," ^ b ^ ")"
  fun format f xs = output (open_out f, showstring "graph{" "
                                        \n        " "}\n" xs)
  (*Post: opens a file f and outputs the list of strings xs to f,
     using showstring to format the output *)
  end
```

We can then define the following structure:

```
structure StringGraph = MkGraph (StringNode)
```

Suppose that we have a graph g with the names of some functional languages in its nodes, as shown in Figure 9.6.

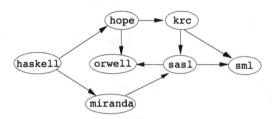

Figure 9.6

This graph can be represented by:

```
val g = addedge ("haskell","hope") (addedge ("haskell","miranda")
        (addedge ("hope","krc")
        (addedge ("hope","orwell") (addedge ("krc", "sasl")
        (addedge ("krc","sml")
        (addedge ("miranda","sasl") (addedge ("sasl","orwell")
        (addedge ("sasl","sml") empty))))))))
```

Now if we open the structures StringGraph and StringNode and evaluate:

```
format "f" (showgraph g)
```

we will find that the file f contains:

```
graph {(haskell,hope)
       (haskell,miranda)
       (hope,krc)
       (hope,orwell)
       (krc,sasl)
       (krc,sml)
       (miranda,sasl)
       (sasl,orwell)
       (sasl,sml)}
```

We can use the structures IntGraph and StringGraph to dynamically test the implementation of the access functions, comparing the results with those predicted by the algebraic specification. Whenever the MkGraph functor is instantiated with a new base type, or a new graph implementation is produced, the tests can be reused to validate the software.

Applying the ADT

Functions which utilise the access procedures (such as the depth first search algorithm, for example) can be encapsulated within a functor which is constrained by a signature called APPS, in which the types of the functions are given, together with their pre- and postconditions:

```
signature APPS =
sig
structure N : NODE
structure G : GRAPH
open N
open G
val depth  :  node list -> graph -> node list -> node list
(*Pre: takes a list with the start node in it, a graph and an
  accumulating parameter which is initially empty
  Post: returns a list of nodes, produces by a depth first traversal
  of the graph from the start node *)
val dfs : graph -> node list list
(*Pre: takes a graph
  Post: returns a list of lists of nodes, produced by a depth first
  traversal of the entire graph *)
val breadth :   node list -> graph -> node list ->  node list
(*Pre: takes a list with the start node in it, a graph and an
  accumulating parameter which is initially empty
  Post: returns a list of nodes, produced by a breadth first traversal
  of the graph from the start node *)
val topsort :  graph -> node list
 (*Pre: takes a graph
  Post : returns a sorted list of nodes *)
end
```

The functor itself is shown below. It includes the searching and sorting algorithms discussed earlier:

```
functor MkApps (structure G : GRAPH) : APPS =
struct
structure G = G
open G

fun depth [] g acc = acc
  | depth (x::xs) g acc = if x member acc then
                              depth xs g acc
                          else
                              depth ((adj x g)@xs) g (acc@[x])

fun dfs g = let val (s::ss) = sources g
              in let fun dfs' g (s::ss) = depth [s] g []::dfs' g ss
                     | dfs' g [] = []
                 in dfs' g (s::ss)
                 end
              end

fun breadth [] g acc = acc
  | breadth (x::xs) g acc = if x  member acc then
                              breadth xs g acc
                          else
                              breadth (xs@(adj x g)) g (acc@[x])
```

```
(*Pre: takes a list of nodes and an accumulating parameter which is
   empty initially
   Post : returns a sorted list of nodes *)
fun tsort [] acc g = acc
  | tsort (x::xs) acc g = if (x member acc) then
                             tsort xs acc g
                          else
                             tsort xs (x::(tsort (adj x g) acc g)) g

fun topsort g = tsort (sources g) [] g

end
```

We can now use this functor to create functions to search and sort graphs of integers and strings, by using the structures presented earlier:

```
structure IntApplications = MkApps (structure Nodes = IntNode
                                             and G = IntGraph)


structure StringApplications = MkApps (structure Nodes = StringNode
                                                and G = StringGraph)
```

EXERCISES 9.1

For the graph g, given below

```
g = addedge (1,2) (addedge (1,4) (addedge (2,3) (addedge (2,5)
    (addedge (3,6)
    (addedge (3,7) (addedge (4,6) (addedge (6,5)
    (addedge (6,7) empty))))))))
```

rewrite each of the following expressions to normal form:

1. depth [1] g []
2. breadth [1] g []
3. topsort g

SUMMARY

- The ADT *graph* consists of a finite set of *nodes* and a set of *edges*, where an edge is a connection between two nodes, together with a number of access functions.
- A *directed graph,* or *digraph*, is defined to be a graph in which each edge has a direction.
- Two nodes are said to be *adjacent*, or *neighbours*, if there is an edge connecting them.
- A *path* is a sequence of nodes $n_1, n_2, ..., n_m$ such that for all i from 1 to $(m-1)$, each pair of nodes (n_i, n_{i+1}) are adjacent.

- A path is *simple* if each of its nodes occurs only once in the sequence. A *cycle* is a path that is simple except that the first and last nodes are the same.
- If a path from a node to itself does not contain any other nodes then it is said to be a *degenerate cycle*.
- A node n_1 is *reachable* from a node n_2 if and only if there exists a path from n_2 to n_1.
- A node n_1 is *directly* reachable from a node n_2 if and only if the two nodes are adjacent and n_1 is the successor of n_2.
- A digraph is *strongly connected* if and only if for each node in the graph there is at least one path to each of the other nodes.
- A tree is an *acyclic* graph, i.e. a graph which does not have any cycles.
- In a depth first traversal of a graph all of the nodes which are on a path from a given starting node are processed. When a node is reached which has no adjacent nodes, or whose adjacent nodes have all been processed, the algorithm backtracks to the last node visited which still has a neighbour to be processed, and a depth first search is started from there. Finally, we reach a point where no more nodes can be reached from any of the processed nodes.
- In a breadth first traversal of a graph, all of the nodes which are adjacent to a given starting node are processed, followed by all of the nodes which are adjacent to one of the processed nodes, and so on.
- A topological sort provides us with a sorting technique for graphs, and produces a sorted list such that if there exists an edge from v to w, then v precedes w in the sorted list. The sort operates by finding a node with no incoming edges. This node is added to the output list and then the rest of the graph (without the node and any edges which were attached to it) is topologically sorted.

APPENDIX 1

A Library of Standard ML Functions

This library contains a number of utility functions written in SML. The functions are listed alphabetically, except for —— (list difference) and ! (list index), which appear at the start.

```
structure Library =
struct

(*Pre: takes 2 lists *)
(*Post: returns the items in the first list which are not in the
  second *)
infix --
fun xs -- [] = xs
  | xs -- (y::ys) = let fun remove [] y = []
                          | remove (x::xs) y = if x = y then xs
                                               else x::(remove xs y)
                    in ((remove xs y) -- ys)
                    end

(*Pre: takes a list and an integer *)
(*Post: returns the item indexed by the integer, where the 1st item in
  the list has index 0 *)
infix !
fun (x::xs) ! 0 = x
  | (x::xs) ! n = xs ! (n-1)

(*Pre: takes 2 integers
  Post: returns their sum *)
fun add (x:int) y = x + y

(*Pre: takes a predicate and a list *)
(*Post: returns true if all of the booleans produced by mapping the
  predicate over the list are true  *)
fun alltrue p [] = true
  | alltrue p (x::xs) = (p x) andalso alltrue p xs

(*Pre:  takes an operator and two arguments
  Post: returns the result of applying the operator to the arguments
  (facilitates the use of sections) *)
fun ap f x y = f (x,y)

(*Pre: takes a list of lists
  Post: returns a single list, the result of concatenating them
  together *)
```

193

```
fun concat [] = []
  | concat (x::xs) = x @ (concat xs)

(*Pre: takes an integer n and a list *)
(*Post: drops the first n items from a list *)
fun drop 0 xs = xs
  | drop n [] = []
  | drop (n:int) (x::xs) = drop (n-1) xs

(*Pre: takes a predicate and a list *)
(*Post: removes the longest initial segment of the list for which the
  predicate holds *)
fun dropwhile p [] = []
  | dropwhile p (x::xs) = if p x then dropwhile p xs
                          else x::xs

(*Pre: takes a predicate and a list *)
(*Post: returns a list for which the predicate holds *)
fun filter p [] = []
  | filter p (x::xs) = if p x then x::filter p xs
                       else filter p xs

(*Pre: takes a dyadic function, a base case and a list *)
(*Post: returns the result of applying the dyadic function f to items
  in the list and the base case *)
fun foldl f a [] = a
  | foldl f a (x::xs) = foldl f (f a x) xs

(*Pre: takes a non-empty list *)
(*Post: applies a dyadic function to 2 items at a time and returns the
  result *)
fun foldl1 f (x::xs) = foldl f x xs

(*Pre: takes a dyadic function, a base case and a list
  Post: returns the result of applying the function to the items in
  the list and the base case *)
fun foldr f a [] = a
  | foldr f a (x::xs) = f x (foldr f a xs)

(*Pre: takes a tuple of 2 items
  Post: returns the first item in the tuple *)
fun fst (x,y) = x

(*Pre: takes a list of pairs
  Post: returns a list consisting of the first item from each pair *)
fun fsts ((a,b)::xs) = a::(fsts xs)
  | fsts [] = []

(*Pre: takes a pair of integers and one other integer *)
(*Post: returns true if x lies between a and b, otherwise false *)
fun inrange (a,b) (x:int) = x >= a andalso x < b

(*Pre: takes an item and a list *)
(*Post: returns true if the given item is in the given list *)
infix member
fun x member xs = exists (ap op= x) xs
```

```
(*Pre: takes 2 integers
  Post: returns the largest *)
fun max2 a (b:int) = if a>=b then a
                     else b

(*Pre: takes a list
  Post: returns the largest item in the list*)
fun max xs = foldl1 max2 xs

(*Pre: takes 3 integers
  Post: returns the largest *)
fun max3 a b (c:int) = max2 a (max2 b c)

(*Pre: takes 2 integers
  Post: returns the smallest *)
fun min2 a (b:int) = if a<=b then a
                     else b

(*Pre: takes a list
  Post: returns the smallest item in the list*)
fun min xs = foldl1 min2 xs

(*Pre: takes a list of items
  Post: returns a list in which all the items are distinct *)
fun  mkset [] = []
  |  mkset (a::x) = a::filter (ap op<> a) (mkset x)

(*Pre: takes a list
  Post: returns the result of reversing the list *)
fun reverse [] = []
  | reverse (x::xs) = reverse xs @ [x]

(*Pre: takes 3 strings and a list of strings *)
(*Post: returns a string, the result of adding fst to the front of the
  given list of string, mid between each list, last at the end and
  joining the lists together *)
fun showstring fst mid last xs = let fun show [] = [last]
                                       |  show [y] = y::[last]
                                       |  show (y::ys) = y::mid::
                                                              (show ys)
                                 in fst ^ implode (show xs)
                                 end

(*Pre: takes a tuple of 2 items
  Post: returns the second item in the tuple *)
fun snd (x,y) = y

(*Pre: takes a list of pairs
  Post: returns a list consisting of the second item from each pair *)
fun snds ((a,b)::xs) = b::(snds xs)
  | snds [] = []

(*Pre: takes a list
  Post: returns the sum of the integers in the list *)
fun sum xs = foldl (ap op+) 0 xs
```

```
(*Pre: takes an integer n and a list *)
(*Post: returns the first n items of a list *)
fun take 0 xs = []
  | take n [] = []
  | take (n:int) (x::xs) = x::take (n-1) xs

(*Pre: takes a predicate and a list *)
(*Post: returns the longest initial segment of the list for which the
  predicate holds *)
fun takewhile p [] = []
  | takewhile p (x::xs) = if p x then x::takewhile p xs
                          else []

(*Pre: takes a predicate, a monadic function and an object  *)
(*Post: applies the function to the object until the predicate is
  true *)
fun until p f x = if p x then x
                  else until p f (f x)

(*Pre: takes a pair of lists *)
(*Post: returns a list of pairs *)
fun zip [] ys = []
  | zip (x::xs) [] = []
  | zip (x::xs) (y::ys) = (x,y)::zip xs ys

end
```

APPENDIX 2

How to Obtain SML

SML is available via ftp (file transfer protocol) or electronic mail from a network library information server called `netlib` at AT&T Bell Laboratories in Murray Hill, New Jersey. The information contained in this appendix was obtained from the information server. The full Internet address is:

`netlib@research.att.com`

This address, which should be understood on all the major networks, refers to a gateway machine, 192.20.225.2. For systems having only uucp (unix-to-unix copy) connections, an alternative address is given below:

`uunet!research!netlib`

For those for whom ftp is more convenient than electronic mail, it is possible to connect to `research.att.com` by logging in as `netlib`. (This is for read-only ftp, not telnet.) Files with names ending in `.z` need to have the UNIX[†] command `uncompress` applied after they have been acquired.

For access from Europe, the duplicate collection in Oslo can be used. This has the following address:

`netlib@nac.no`

For the Pacific, the following address (located at the University of Wollongong, NSW, Australia) can be used:

`netlib@draci.cs.uow.edu.au`

OBTAINING SML USING ELECTRONIC MAIL

To obtain an index of what is available from the network library via electronic mail, the following command can be used:

`mail netlib@research.att.com`

---

† UNIX is a registered trademark of UNIX System Laboratories, Inc.

The subject line is ignored, and so can be left empty. Table A2.1 shows the possible contents of the mail message, and the responses from the network library. Each command should be typed on a separate line.

Table A2.1

Command	Response
send index	returns the index of the contents of the whole network library
send directory for ml	returns a list of file sizes, dates and times of all the files in the ml library
mailsize 100k	sets the partitioning size which will be used for the reply
send ml	returns the whole ml library
send file f from ml	returns the file *f* from the ml library
quit	indicates the end of the request (optional)

Examples

The entry for SML in the index is as follows:

```
lib        ml

for        Standard ML of New Jersey
#          (programming language compiler)
#          uuencoded compressed tar files

editor     Dave MacQueen
master     research.att.com
```

Table A2.2 contains an excerpt from the output of sending mail to netlib@research.att.com with the message:

```
send directory for ml
```

Table A2.2

636303	Apr 17	17:36	tools
589	Apr 17	17:35	index
4056	Dec 12	1991	readme
899766	Dec 12	1991	testing
1310619	Dec 12	1991	src
1497866	Dec 12	1991	mo.vax
2298234	Dec 12	1991	mo.sparc
1979336	Dec 12	1991	mo.mips1
1951918	Dec 12	1991	mo.mipsb
1401724	Dec 12	1991	mo.m68
885415	Dec 12	1991	lib
1205863	Dec 12	1991	doc

To obtain the file called index from the network library , send the message:

```
send file index from ml
```

This produces the output shown in Table A2.3.

Table A2.3

file	ml/readme
for	description of Standard ML of New Jersey distribution
file	ml/src
for	compiler source
file	ml/lib
for	contributed library of sml software
file	ml/tools
for	SML tools like mlyacc
file	ml/doc
for	documentation
file	ml/mo.m68
for	object files for MC680x0 (Sun 3, NeXT, HP, etc)
file	ml/mo.vax
for	object files for vax
file	ml/mo.sparc
for	object files for sparc-based machines (Sun 4, Sparcstation)
file	ml/mo.mipsb
for	object files for bigendian MIPS processors
file	ml/mo.mipsl
for	object files for little-endian MIPS processors

Bibliography

Abelson, H., Sussman, G.J. and Sussman, J. (1987) *Structure and Interpretation of Computer Programs*, MIT Press.

Adelson-Velskii, G.M. and Landis, Y.M. (1962) An algorithm for the organisation of information, *Soviet Math. Dokl.* (English translation), **3**, 1259–1262.

Aho, A.V., Hopcroft, J. E. and Ullman, J. D. (1974) *The Design and Analysis of Computer Algorithms*, Addison Wesley.

Andrew, D. and Ince, D. (1991) *Practical Formal Methods with VDM*, McGraw-Hill.

Barendregt, H.P. (1984) *The Lambda Calculus—Its Syntax and Semantics,* North Holland.

Bayer, R. and McCreight, C. (1972) Organization and maintenance of large ordered indexes, *Acta Informatica*, **1**, No. 3, 173–189.

Bell, D., Morrey, I. and Pugh, J. (1992) *Software Engineering, A Programming Approach*, Prentice Hall (2nd ed.)

Biggerstaff, T.J. and Perlis, A.J. (editors) (1989) *Software Reusability, (1), Concepts and Models*, ACM Press.

Bird, R. and Wadler, P. (1988) *Introduction to Functional Programming,* Prentice-Hall International.

Bjorner, D. and Jones, C.B. (1982) *Formal Specification and Software Development*, Prentice-Hall International.

Boehm, B.W., Gray, T.E. and Seewaldt, T. (1984) Prototyping versus specifying: a multi-project experiment, *IEEE Trans. Software Engineering*, **10** (3), 290–303.

Burge, W.H. (1975) *Recursive Programming Techniques*, Addison Wesley.

Burstall, R.M. and Goguen, J.A. (1977) Putting theories together to make specifications, *Proceedings 5th Annual Joint Conference on Artificial Intelligence*, Cambridge, Mass., 1045–1058.

Burstall, R.M. and Goguen, J.A. (1979) The semantics of CLEAR, a specification language, *Abstract Software Specification, Proceedings 1979*, LNCS 86, D. Bjorner, ed., Springer-Verlag.

Burstall, R.M., MacQueen, D.B. and Sanella, D.T. (1980) HOPE: An experimental applicative language, *Proceedings 1st International LISP Conference*, Stanford, California, pp. 136–143.

Burton, F.W. (1982) An efficient functional implementation of FIFO queues, *Information Processing Letters*, **14**, 205–206.

Cardelli, L. and Wegner, P. (1985) On understanding types, data abstraction, and poly-morphism, *Computer Surveys*, 17 (4), 471–522.

Cohen, B., Harwood, W.T. and Jackson, M.I. (1986) *The Specification of Complex Systems*, Addison Wesley.

Cormen, T. H., Leiserson, C. E. and Rivest, R. L. (1990) *Introduction to Algorithms*, MIT Press & McGraw-Hill.

Curry, H.B. and Feys, R. (1958) *Combinatory Logic I*, North-Holland.

Darlington, J. (1982) Program transformation, in [*Darlington et al*, 1982], pp. 193–209.

Darlington, J. and Burstall, R.M. (1976) A System which automatically improves programs, *Acta Informatica*, **6**, 41–60.

Darlington, J., Henderson, P. and Turner, D.A. (editors) (1982) *Functional Programming and its Applications: An Advanced Course*, Cambridge University Press.

David, E.E. (1969) *Software Engineering*, Naur, P. and Randell, B., ed., NATO Scientific Affairs Division, Belgium.

Davie, A.J.T. (1992) *An Introduction to Functional Programming Systems*, Cambridge University Press.

Downs, E., Clare, P. and Coe, I. (1988) *Structured Systems Analysis and Design Method*, Prentice Hall.

Ellis, R. (1990) *Data Abstraction and Program Design*, Pitman.

Field, A.J. and Harrison, P.G. (1988) *Functional Programming*, Addison Wesley.

Fraser, A.G. (1969) *Software Engineering*, Naur, P. and Randell, B., ed., NATO Scientific Affairs Division, Belgium.

Friedman, D.P, Wand, M. and Haynes, C.T. (1992) *Essentials of Programming Languages*, MIT Press.

Furtado, A.L. and Maibaum, T.S.E. (1985) An informal approach to formal (algebraic) specifications, *The Computer Journal*, **28** (1), 59–67.

Gehani, N. and McGettrick, A.D. (editors) (1986) *Software Specification Techniques*, Addison Wesley.

Glaser, H., Hankin, C. and Till, D. (1984) *Principles of Functional Programming*, Prentice-Hall.

Goguen, J.A. and Winkler, T. (1988) Introducing OBJ3, *SRI-CSL-88-9*, SRI International.

Goguen, J.A. (1989a) Principles of parameterized programming, in *Software Reusability, 1, Concepts and Methods*, ed. T. Biggerstaff and A. Perlis, ACM Press.

Goguen, J.A. (1989b) Higher order functions considered unnecessary for higher-order programming, *SRI-CSL-88-1*, Project No. 1243, SRI International, July 1989.

Goguen, J.A., Thatcher, J.W. and Wagner, E.G. (1978) An initial algebra approach to the specification, correctness and implementation of abstract data types, *Current Trends in Programming Methodology, 4, Data Structuring*, Prentice-Hall.

Goguen, J.A. and Tardo, J. (1979) An introduction to OBJ: a language for writing and testing software specifications, *Specification of Reliable Software*, M. Zelkowitz, ed., IEEE Press, New York, 170–189. Reprinted in *Software Specification Techniques*, N. Gehani and A. McGettrick, ed., Addison Wesley, pp. 391–420, 1986.

Goldberg, A. and Robson, D. (1983) *Smalltalk-80 - The Language and its Implementation*, Addison Wesley.

Gordon, M.J.C., Milner, R., Morris, L., Newey, M.C. and Wadsworth, C.P. (1978) A metalanguage for interactive proof in LCF, *Proceedings 5th ACM Symposium on Principles of Programming Languages*, Tuscon.

Gries, D. (1981) *The Science of Programming*, Springer-Verlag.

Guttag, J.V. (1975) *The Specification and Application to Programming of Abstract Data Types*, PhD Thesis, Toronto.

Guttag, J.V. (1977) Abstract data types and the development of data structures, *Communications of the ACM*, **20**, 397–404.

Guttag, J.V. (1978) The algebraic specification of abstract data types, *Acta Informatica*, **10**, No. 1, 27–52.

Guttag, J.V. (1980) Notes on type abstraction (second version), *IEEE Transactions on Software Engineering*, **SE-6**, No.1, 13–23.

Guttag, J.V. (1982) Some notes on putting formal specifications to productive use, *Science of Computer Programming*, **2**(1), 53–68.

Guttag, J.V., Horning, J.J. and Wing, J.M. (1985) Larch in five easy pieces, *Digital SRC Research Report*, **5**, July 1985.

Guttag, J.V., Horning, J.J. and Wing, J.M. (1985) The Larch family of specification languages, *IEEE Software*, **2** (4).

Guttag, J.V., Horowitz, E. and Musser, D.R. (1978) Abstract data types and software validation, *Communications of the ACM*, **21**, 1048–1064.

Hall, A. (1990) Seven myths of formal methods, *IEEE Software*, (9), 11–19.

Harper, R. (1986) Introduction to Standard ML, *Edinburgh University Internal Report LFCS-86-14*.

Harper, R, MacQueen, D. and Milner, R. (1986) Standard ML, *Edinburgh University Internal Report LFCS-86-2*.

Harrison, R. (1989) *Abstract Data Types in Modula-2*, John Wiley.

Henderson, P. (1980) *Functional Programming Application and Implementation*, Prentice-Hall International.

Henson, M.C. (1987) *Elements of Functional Programming Languages*, Blackwell Scientific Publications.

Hille, R.F. (1988) *Data Abstraction and Program Development using Pascal*, Advances in Computer Science Series, Prentice Hall.

Hindley, J.R. (1969) The principal type scheme of an object in combinatory logic, *Transactions of the American Mathematical Society*, **146**, 29–60.

Hoare, C.A.R. (1969) The axiomatic basis of computer programming, *Communications of the ACM*, **12**, 576–583.

Hoare, C.A.R. (1972) Proofs of correctness of data representations, *Acta Informatica*, **1**, No. 1, 271–281.

Holyer, I. (1991) *Functional Programming with Miranda*, Pitman.

Horowitz, E. and Sahni, S. (1976) *Fundamentals of Data Structures*, Pitman.

Hudak, P. (1989) Conception, evolution, and application of functional programming languages, *ACM Computing Surveys*, **21** (3), 359–411.

Hudak, P. and Fasel, J.H. (1992) A gentle introduction to Haskell, *ACM Sigplan Notices*, **27** (5), 1–53.

Hudak, P. and Wadler, P. (editors) (1990) Report on the Programming Language Haskell, *Yale University Technical Report and SIGPLAN Notices*, **27** (5).

Hughes, R.J.M. (1989) Why functional programming matters, *The Computer Journal*, **32** (2), 98–107.

Jones, C.B. (1986) *Systematic Software Development Using VDM*, Prentice-Hall International.

Jones, C.B. (1990) *Systematic Software Development Using VDM*, Prentice-Hall International (2nd ed.).

Kaes, S. (1988) Parametric Overloading in Polymorphic Programming Languages, *2nd European Symposium on Programming*, Nancy, Springer-Verlag LNCS 300, pp. 131–144.

Kaldewaij, A. (1990) *Programming: The Derivation of Algorithms*, Prentice-Hall International.

Knuth, D.E. (1973) *The Art of Computer Programming: Sorting and Searching*, Vol. 3, Addison Wesley.

Kruse, R.L. (1987) *Data Structures and Program Design*, Prentice-Hall International.

Liskov, B. and Guttag, J. (1986) *Abstraction and Specification in Program Development*, MIT Press.

Liskov, B.H. and Zillies, S.N. (1975) Specification techniques for data abstractions, *IEEE Transactions on Software Engineering*, **1**, No. 1, 7–19.

MacLennan, B.J. (1990) *Functional Programming, Practice and Theory*, Addison Wesley.

MacQueen, D.B. (1984) Modules for Standard ML, *Proceedings of the 1984 ACM Symposium on Lisp and Functional Programming*, Austin, Texas, pp. 198–207.

MacQueen, D.B. (1988) An implementation of Standard ML modules, *Proceedings of the 1988 ACM Conference on Lisp and Functional Programming*, Snowbird, Utah, pp. 212–23.

Martin, J.J. (1986) *Data Types and Data Structures*, Prentice-Hall International.

Mills, H.D. and Linger, R.C. (1986) Data structured programming: program design without arrays and pointers, *IEEE Trans. Software Engineering*, **SE 12**, 192–7.

Milner, R. (1978) A theory of type polymorphism in programming, *Journal of Computer and System Science*, **17**, 349–75.

Milner, R. and Tofte, M. (1991) *Commentary of Standard ML*, MIT Press.

Milner, R., Tofte, M. and Harper, R. (1990) *The Definition of Standard ML*, MIT Press.

Mitchell, R. (1992) *Abstract Data Types and Modula-2*, Prentice-Hall International.

Morgan, C.C. (1990) *Programming from Specifications,* Prentice-Hall International.

Morris, J.M. (1990) Programs from Specifications, *Formal Development of Programs and Proofs*, E.W. Dijkstra ed., Addison Wesley.

Paulson, L.C. (1991) *ML for the Working Programmer*, Cambridge University Press.

Pomberger, G. (1984) *Software Engineering with Modula-2*, Prentice-Hall International.

Reade, C. (1989) *Elements of Functional Programming*, Addison Wesley.

Rumblaugh, J., Blaha, M., Premerlani, W., Eddy, F. and Lorensen, W. (1991) *Object-Oriented Modelling and Design*, Prentice-Hall International.

Sannella, D. (1991) Formal program development in Extended ML for the working programmer, *Proc. 3rd BCS/FACS Workshop on Refinement*, Hursley Park, Springer Workshops in Computing, pp. 99–130.

Sannella, D. and Tarlecki, A. (1984) Program specification and development in Standard ML, *Conference Record of the 12th Annual ACM Symposium on Principles of Programming Languages*, pp. 67–77.

Sebesta, R.W. (1989) *Concepts of Programming Languages*, Addison Wesley.

Sedgewick, R. (1988) *Algorithms*, Addison Wesley (2nd ed.).

Sethi, R. (1988) *Programming Languages: Concepts and Constructs*, Addison Wesley.

Stansifer, R. (1992) *ML Primer*, Prentice Hall.

Stevens, W.P., Myers, G.J. and Constantine, L.L. (1974) Structured design, *IBM Systems Journal No. 2*.

Stoy, J.E. (1981) *Denotational Semantics: The Scott-Strachey Approach to Programming Language Theory*, The MIT Press. (1st ed. 1977).

Stroupstrup, B. (1985) *The C++ Programming Language*, Addison Wesley.

Stubbs, D.F. and Webre, N.W. (1987) *Data Structures with Abstract Data Types and Modula-2*, Brooks Cole.

Tenenbaum, A.M. and Augenstein, M.J. (1986) *Data Structures Using Pascal*, Prentice-Hall International.

Thompson, S. (1991) *Type Theory and Functional Programming*, Addison Wesley.

Turner, D.A. (1982) Recusion Equations as a Programming Language, in [*Darlington et al*, 1982], 1–28.

Turner, D.A. (1985a) Miranda: a non-strict functional language with polymorphic types, *Functional Programming Languages and Computer Architecture*, Nancy, France, Springer-Verlag LNCS 201, pp. 1–16.

Turner, D.A. (1985b) Functional programs as executable specifications, *Mathematical Logic and Programming Languages,* C.A.R. Hoare and J.C. Shepherdson, ed., Prentice-Hall International.

Turner, D.A. (1986) An overview of Miranda, *ACM Sigplan Notices,* **21** (12).

Turner, R. (1991) *Constructive Foundations for Functional Languages,* McGraw-Hill Book Company.

U.S. Department of Defense (1983) *Reference Manual for the Ada Programming Language,* ANSI/MIL-STD-1815A.

Watt, D.A. (1990) *Programming Language Concepts and Paradigms,* Prentice-Hall International.

Weyuker, E.J. (1982) On testing non-testable programs, *The Computer Journal,* **25** (4), 465–70.

Wikström, A. (1987) *Functional Programming Using Standard ML,* Prentice-Hall International.

Williams, J.W.J. (1964) Heapsort, *Communications of the ACM,* **7**, No. 6, 347–8.

Willis, C. and Paddon, D. (1992) *Abstraction and Specification in Modula-2,* Pitman.

Wirth, N. (1971. Program Development by stepwise refinement, *Communications of the ACM,* **14**, No. 4, 221–7.

Wirth, N. (1986) *Algorithms and Data Structure*s, Prentice-Hall International.

Wirth, N. (1988) *Programming in Modula-2,* Springer-Verlag (4th Ed.).

Index